IRELAND'S GHOSTS, LEGENDS, & LORE

We do lie beneath the grass

In the moonlight, in the shade

Of the yew-tree. They that pass

Hear us not. We are afraid

They would envy our delight,

In our graves by glow-worm night.

Come follow us, and smile as we;

We sail to the rock in the ancient waves,

Where the snow falls by thousands into the sea,

And the drowned and the shipwrecked have happy graves.

—Thomas Lovell Beddoes
"Sibilla's Dirge"

Knockma Tree. *Courtesy of Ciaran McHugh.*

Ireland's Ghosts, Legends, & Lore

E. Ashley Rooney
Photography by Ciaran McHugh

Schiffer Publishing Ltd ®

4880 Lower Valley Road • Atglen, PA 19310

DEDICATION

To my editor, Dinah Roseberry.
She catches my gaffes, spurs me on,
and is a joy to work with.

Schiffer Books are available at special discounts for bulk purchases for sales promotions or premiums. Special editions, including personalized covers, corporate imprints, and excerpts can be created in large quantities for special needs. For more information contact the publisher:

Published by Schiffer Publishing, Ltd.
4880 Lower Valley Road
Atglen, PA 19310
Phone: (610) 593-1777; Fax: (610) 593-2002
E-mail: Info@schifferbooks.com.

For the largest selection of fine reference books on this and related subjects,
please visit our website at
www.schifferbooks.com.

We are always looking for people to write books on new and related subjects.
If you have an idea for a book, please contact us at
proposals@schifferbooks.com.

This book may be purchased from the publisher.
Please try your bookstore first.
You may write for a free catalog.

Other Schiffer Books By The Author:

Berkshire Ghosts, Legends & Lore
978-0-7643-2797-1 $14.95

Cambridge, Massachusetts Ghosts, Legends, and Lore
978-0-7643-3255-5 $14.99

Empire State Ghosts Legends: New York Legends and Lore
978-0-7643-3418-4 $14.99

Haunted London: English Ghosts, Legends, and Lore
978-0-7643-3149-7 $14.99

Lexington, Bedford, and Concord: Ghosts, Legends, and Lore
978-0-7643-3115-2 $14.99

Washington D.C.: Ghosts, Legends, and Lore
978-0-7643-2961-6 $14.99

Scottish Ghosts
978-0-7643-3990-5 $16.99

Front cover image: The medieval church and graveyard at Carraigin were built within the boundaries of an earlier ecclesiastical enclosure. It is not known when exactly the original church was built, but it was recorded as being in ruins by 1641. A children's burial ground has been located within the walls of the ruined church. Children's burial grounds were generally used for burying stillborn or unbaptized children as they were not permitted to be buried on consecrated church grounds. *Courtesy of Ciaran McHugh.*

Copyright © 2013 by E. Ashley Rooney
Photos by Ciaran McHugh unless otherwise noted

Library of Congress Control Number: 2013941722

Designed by Mark David Bowyer
Type set in Abaddon / Zurich BT

ISBN: 978-0-7643-4508-1
Printed in China

Contents

Acknowledgments

Many of us don't quite understand ghosts. In this book, I have told or retold these Irish ghost stories, trying from my comfortable place in the twenty-first century to make sense of the past. Throughout the work, I have endeavored to be as true to historical fact as possible. I was most fortunate to find Ciaran and his wonderful images of Ireland; my dear friend Paul Doherty was able to supply me with the elegant Giant's Causeway; and Barbara Purchia was a kind editor.

Introduction

Any visitor to Ireland can soon appreciate why the Irish have such a belief in the forces of the unknown. Known to be inhabited for at least 9,000 years, Ireland's history is extremely complex. Legends and myths have been a part of daily life since the Celtics began to arrive by boat around 400 BCE.

The Celts worshipped many gods and looked to the druids for healing and magic. Many of the old beliefs still linger. Even today the influence of fairies is still evident. Ghosts range from the supernatural to modern superstition. Banshees whose cry can be heard whenever death is about to occur are still talked about. Spirits frequent castles, manors, and other institutions, while some of the scariest of Ireland's spooks still lie in wait.

Irish bogs are famous for accumulating peat, a deposit of dead plant material, which is often used as fuel. The cutting of peat (called "turf" when cut) for fuel began in the seventeenth century and continued at an increasing rate until the mid-twentieth century. At one time, a large part of Ireland was covered in bogs, which were considered treacherous places to walk. *Courtesy of Ciaran McHugh.*

The Early Centuries

The Celts were well established in Ireland by about 150 BCE, resisting challenges from many newcomers and establishing a culture, which still can be seen today. They dominated the culture for the next thousand years, and their language forms the basis of modern Gaelic or Irish. Their typical settlement was the ring fort, which can still be found throughout Ireland. Legend tells us that Saint Patrick established Christianity in the fifth century and expelled all the snakes. He is reported to have established 300 churches. Today, Irish people throughout the world celebrate the day of his death: March 17. As the influence of the new religion grew, the Celtic gods gradually became heroes rather than deities. From the fifth to seventh centuries, Ireland was a significant center of Christianity in northwest Europe.

The Vikings began attacking Ireland in 795 AD and were finally defeated in 1014. Many Vikings remained in the Emerald Isle, and their culture merged with the native Irish culture. By now, Ireland had a vibrant native culture with its own literature and language, a strong Christian faith, and many cultural traditions. The first grammar to be written in Western Europe was produced here and art and architecture blossomed. The political scene, however, was dominated by war, murder, and general mayhem, as the Irish rulers waged long and complicated struggles, striving to control as much territory as possible.

In 1166, the Anglo-Normans invaded. In 1171, King Henry II of England held the titles King of England and King of Ireland. Within eighty years, three-quarters of Ireland was under Britain's control, which continued for more than seven centuries. The Anglo-Normans established a central government, introduced English law, developed a monetary system, and created a parliament with representatives from each country. They increasingly integrated with the local Celtic nobility through intermarriage and are said by many to have become more Irish than the Irish themselves.

Although the Irish chieftains lost power, life became more settled. Towns were established around Norman castles, and trade flourished. The English kings were too busy battling elsewhere to get involved in Ireland, but they would intervene when the lords threatened to become too powerful. By 1250, the Normans occupied the best Irish lands – over three-quarters of Ireland – leaving the hills, bogs, and woods to the natives. Many lords designated property to become towns near their castles.

The English settlers were always insecure, while the native Irish gentry and the lower classes stirred with rebellion. When the Norman nobles, most notably the Earls of Desmond and Kildare, began to openly disobey and even disavow the English monarch, the English introduced the Statutes of Kilkenney in 1366, which prohibited, among other things, all intermarriage and outlawed the use of the Irish language, dress, and names.

Colonization of Ireland

Beginning in the sixteenth century, Great Britain's political and cultural colonization of Ireland intensified, culminating in 1801 in its absorption of Ireland. During this time, there were the Gaelic Irish, who wanted to run their own affairs; the Anglo-Irish, the descendants of the early Norman settlers who had become a part of the Irish society; and the settlers and the representatives of the English crown. For more than a century, religious discord, outbreaks of armed rebellion, social and political instability, and famines plagued the nation and its people.

Henry VIII and Elizabeth I began the conquest of Ireland in earnest as they worked to establish a Protestant England. By the 1590s, Queen Elizabeth had successfully subdued Ireland except in Ulster, which remained entirely Gaelic in government and culture. The Earl of Tyrone, Hugh O'Neill, led an unsuccessful rebellion, which culminated in the Treaty of Mellifont in 1603 and the end of the old Irish world. In 1607, he and ninety of Ulster's leading nobles went into voluntary exile on the continent. Their estates were forfeited to the Crown and settled with loyal Protestants from Great Britain.

The "Flight of the Earls" is generally taken as the death of the old Gaelic order. It left Ulster leaderless, which provided the English with the opportunity to deprive the Irish Catholics of their land and establish Protestant English colonists on the confiscated lands. The early sixteenth century saw thousands arrive from England and the Scottish lowlands, putting a large number of loyal British subjects in Ireland in the hopes of guaranteeing the state's security. These Protestants brought their own institutions and traditions and were expected to bring in Protestant tenant farmers and build defenses for the residents' safety. In practice, they accepted Irish tenants because it was more profitable. As a result, Ulster became a province with two antagonistic populations: Catholic vs. Protestant. From that point on, the superior force of Protestant England dominated Catholic Ireland. One spoke Gaelic; the other spoke English. Religion fanned the national animosities, thus intensifying the antipathy on both sides.

In 1641, the Ulster Irish rebelled, destroying the English properties, stripping many of their clothing and possessions, and killing the settlers. Seven years of confusion ensued, ending when the Protestant Oliver Cromwell and his Parliamentarians deposed and executed Charles I and established the Commonwealth. Cromwell immediately set about to stamp out all opposition to the English government and Catholicism in the Irish colony. He gave seized Irish lands to the Protestant soldiers who had served under him.

When James II and his army were defeated at the Battle of the Boyne in 1690, it was the end for the Irish Catholics. The Protestants controlled Ireland, while the Catholics, who were in the majority, endured wholesale oppression and the Irish landowning aristocracy ceased to exist. In 1707, under the reign of Queen Anne, the Act of Union united the crowns of England and Scotland and the constituent countries became "The Kingdom of Great Britain."

To maintain Protestant supremacy, Penal Laws were established that persecuted Irish Catholics. Among other things, they excluded Catholics from public life, purchasing land, voting, and joining the army, as well as outlawing Catholic worship. Since Catholic schools were also forbidden, many Irish children had no formal education or attended Protestant schools. By the late 1770s, Catholics, although they comprised about seventy-five percent of the population, owned only five percent of the land. Gradually, however, the Protestant settlers became Irish people with their own interests at heart. Eventually, the English began to recognize a limited form of Irish independence, although the Irish ministers still represented the Crown, rather than the Irish people.

The French Revolution led to pockets of rebellion. In 1798, inspired by the American and French revolutions, the Irish staged a major rebellion against British rule. Widespread hangings and floggings soon followed as the rebellion was brutally squashed. Alarmed by the prospect of a bloody revolution, given the success of the American Revolution, the English government enacted an Act of Union in 1800 that united Britain and Ireland under one king and parliament. Catholics were still restricted from owning land, undertaking certain jobs, and representing Ireland in the British parliament.

In the first half of the nineteenth century, the upper and middle class in Ireland were Protestants, who largely supported union with Britain, while the Catholics, who accounted for almost eighty percent of the population, were generally poor, unschooled, rural laborers. The average Catholic farmer lived in poverty on less than ten acres and could be evicted on short notice at the whim of the landlord, his agent, or middleman. For many Irish, the potato was their only food, and when the crop was good the average Irish adult male ate ten pounds of potatoes a day. The mutual antipathy between the two groups had developed to bitter antagonism when the Great Famine first occurred in September 1845. Thousands perished.

Emigration and the Push for Independence

The famine forced many Irish to immigrate to other countries and gave a greater impetus to the nationalist movement. About twenty-five percent of Ireland's Catholic, Irish-speaking, and illiterate population fled in a ten-year period. After the famine, emigration was an accepted way of life for working-class Irish without access to land. They made the trip to England, the United States, Canada, Australia, and other countries and found a new way of life.

The bulk of the merchant classes in Ireland were centered in Ulster and were largely Protestant, the descendants of the planters settled in Ireland under Elizabeth I. As industry began to flourish by the end of the nineteenth century, the Ulster Protestants saw their future prosperity in terms of remaining part of Britain. Concurrently, the Catholic majority supported the Irish nationalist movement, Sinn Fein. In 1916, in the middle of World War I, about 100 Sinn Finn militiamen led the Easter Rising. In all, about 1,500 men took part in the rebellion, which began on Easter Monday; by Friday, the center of Dublin lay in ruins. The leaders were executed. Civil war became inevitable.

In 1921, Ireland was divided into Northern Ireland and the Irish Free State, which became the Republic of Ireland in 1949.

Today, Ireland has two governments. Northern Ireland is part of the United Kingdom and is represented in the British House of Commons. The rest of Ireland is an independent republic with its own constitution and democratic system of government. In 2010, the Republic and Northern Ireland had 6.3 million people, almost 3 million less than Ireland's population before the Great Famine. Because its many problems caused generations of Irish to emigrate, their legacy is seen worldwide.

GHOSTS

This house is surrounded by supernatural events. The son of the household, Owen, toured Egypt and Syria as an antiquarian, and, in 1855, brought back several artifacts to his home, then known as Seafield. Shortly after, a violent poltergeist, who would spend the night smashing any breakables throughout the house, appeared. These supernatural events resulted in the demise of Seafield House, as the family couldn't convince the domestic staff to return to work there. The name of the house was changed to Lisheen House in 1899; it was sold in 1938, cleared of all its contents, and left to go to ruin. In summer 2007, Lisheen House parachuted to worldwide fame when it was featured on the American paranormal reality television series *Ghost Hunters*. The show tells the story of Owen Phibbs' alleged grave robbing in the Middle East and suggests that unearthly sounds can be still be heard from the basement at Lisheen House. *Courtesy of Ciaran McHugh.*

Abhartach

In the north Derry area is a grave known locally as "The Giant's Grave." During the fifth and sixth centuries, this area consisted of many small kingdoms, each with its own local ruler. Abhartach, according to tradition, was one of these chieftains. He was small, some say a dwarf, and he was a powerful wizard and a brutal king. His subjects hated him, but they were too frightened to kill him themselves because of his alleged magic powers.

They might not have had the courage to kill him, but they did have the money to hire another chieftain named Cathain to slay Abhartach. He did so, burying him standing up, which is the appropriate burial for an Irish chieftain. Everyone was thrilled, but the next day, Abhartach reappeared, demanding a bowl of human blood from his subjects to "sustain his vile corpse." His subjects went to Cathain, begging him once again to rid them of this tyrannical king. Cathain killed him again and reburied him, but the next day, much to everyone's dismay, the awful corpse returned, demanding another bowl of blood.

Realizing that he had to do more than just kill Abhartach, Cathain consulted with wise men, who told him that Abhartach was not completely dead, nor could he be killed because of his magic powers. "Through his devilish arts," they said, "he has become one of the undead. Moreover, he is a drinker of human blood, a vampire. He cannot actually be slain – but he can be restrained." He was in a state of suspension, one of the walking dead, who would torment people until the end of time unless he was killed forever. The wisemen instructed Cathain to kill him with a sword made of yew wood, bury him upside down, place thorns around his grave, and put a great stone directly on top of him. Only then could the wizard be restrained in his grave. Should the stone be lifted, however, they warned the loathsome king would be free to walk the earth and feed his blood lust once more.

Cathain followed their instructions precisely, and even built a sepulcher over the gravesite. Today, the sepulcher is gone, although the villagers say that one massive capstone remains over the burial site.

In 1997, when the land was being cleared, workmen who attempted to cut down the thorn tree arching across Abhartach's grave allegedly had their chain saw malfunction three times. While attempting to lift the great stone, a steel chain snapped, cutting a laborer's hand. The blood soaked the ground. Although there has been no talk of vampires in the area, not many locals will approach the site in the dark.

Avenge Me

The ruined old fortress at Kerrigan's Keep is known as a dreadful place. The walls are splotched in pale grey-green and beribboned with smoke stain. This endless stone maze has walls that seem to shift and change behind you. The stone walls seem to drip blood in some of the rooms, and the windows are slits staring back at you.

The 1400s

In 1360, Roe Kerrigan built the looming fortress. He raised his family within its walls. Any clashes were confined to raids and counter-raids, aimed at running off the other clan's cattle and any other chattel that they might find. When Kerrigan's son married Marra Dartry, life changed, and the relative calm that reigned in these hills was over. Marra knew that land meant power and she was determined to have both. She killed anyone who stood in her way. Farms and castles – she took them all. No one escaped. There was no doubt who wore the pants in Kerrigan's Keep.

Marra met her match in her neighbor, Ordlin O'Downey, who decided a woman would not beat him. He raised an army, which completely routed hers in a battle to the death. She returned to her dark and dreary fortress to recover from her wounds, raise her three sons, and feel the defeat gnawing inside her – a black worm in her soul. Night after night, she sat in the Great Hall, looking at the flames of the fire, summoning all the reasons why she hated Ordlin and plotting her revenge. As gout and brittle bones took their toll, she aired her dusty feud, forgetting nothing and forgiving less. Her toothless mouth shook as she told her three sons why she hated Ordlin and how she would get vengeance.

When her two eldest sons were in their late teens, she decided that the time had come to go to war. "No one vanquishes me. I will fight that man and win," she announced. On hearing this, Ordlin summoned most of the great chieftains in the West of Ireland, and they raised a great army.

In the following weeks, both armies resounded to the clashing of swords , the clanging of hammers, and the furious barking of hounds as they prepared for battle. Marra's sons decided their best strategy was to sleep in the Bog of Bealaclugga the night before the battle. The night was one of moonlight and shadows and dank, grey fog. Wisps of pale mist drifted throughout the bog as Ordlin's army drew near. The tread of many horses, the rattle of swords and spears, the murmur of human voices signaled their approach, but Marra's soldiers slumbered on until Ordlin's men and horses emerged to wake the sleeping army. Trumpets blew, and Marra's men buckled their sword belts as they ran to fight. By noon it was all over. Marra Kerrigan and her two elder sons lay dead. Severed at the shoulder, her right arm still grasped in its hand the bronze sword of the Kerrigans, carried only by its chieftain. Using her left index finger, she had written "Avenge Me – Never Cease" in her own blood on the edge of her tunic.

Her youngest son, Dulin, became the master of Kerrigan's Keep. Although he appeared to be mild mannered, Dulin ruled his lands with authority. Nothing escaped his attention. No longer too small or too young or the baby of the family, he remembered his mother's final words. There in his Great Hall, along with the gleam of sword and lance, armor and helmets, was a banner high on the wall emblazoned with "Avenge Me – Never Cease" in blood-red letters.

The years passed, and those who had been involved grew old. Close to ninety years of age, Ordlin's eyes stood out in his bony, almost skeletal head. He was old, and he felt old. His head shook and his fingers twitched up and down. Before he died, he wanted to see his daughter one last time. He decided to travel with a small group of men at arms and a few women of his household to her home. His journey took him past Kerrigan's Keep. Unfortunately, the rains had begun, floods destroyed the bridges, and the roads were impassible. Hearing about the difficulties of Ordlin's trip, Dulin invited him and his companions to stay at Kerrigan's Keep.

Ordlin considered the invitation carefully. They were both much older; what would be the point of carrying a grudge for this long? Let bygones be bygones, he said to himself. The Irish code of hospitality is well known. Once he and his men had eaten Dulin's bread and salt, they would have the guest right and the laws of hospitality would protect them. Outside the wind was roaring, the rain came in torrents; his bones were aching. Inside at the Keep would be the leaping flames of a wood and peat fire in a fireplace maybe twelve feet wide. Ordlin thankfully accepted Dulin's offer.

The second night of his visit, Dulin invited Ordlin and his companions to attend a great banquet to celebrate the birthday of his oldest son, Cullen. Telling his men to lay aside their armor, Ordlin was seated at the right hand of Dulin, who dedicated himself to his needs throughout the meal. The juggler kept a cascade of burning clubs spinning through the air, dancers waved brilliantly colored streamers, and the singers told stories through their songs. Dulin was the soul of courtesy, talking to Ordlin, sharing little bits of local gossip, and pouring him more wine. All the while the food came and went. Salmon fresh from the river and wild boar followed a thick soup of barley and venison. Later came baked apples fragrant with cinnamon, spices, and clotted cream.

As midnight approached, the entertainers withdrew, followed by the women and children of the Kerrigan household. Ordlin rose to join them. "I'm an old man and tired," he declared, his chin trembling slightly. "Let the young ones stay up and celebrate." As he turned toward the door, it banged shut, and iron bars clanged into place. Turning, Ordlin heard Dulin draw his blade from its scabbard. Suddenly, Dulan's soldiers wielding double-handed battle swords swarmed into the Great Hall, where they massacred every man and woman in Ordlin's party. As the slaughter took place, Dulin just sat, caressing his sword, hunched in his place, muttering, "Avenge me – never cease, avenge me – never cease."

Behind the Great Hall is a tall, narrow room. After the slaughter, the Kerrigans set to their tasks in a sort of frenzied domesticity. They removed the stones of the floor, dug pits, and tossed Ordlin and his companions into this makeshift grave. They replaced the floor stones, sealed up the empty room, and erased all signs that it even existed.

The 1700s

Centuries passed. Then, in the 1730s, Michael Dartry, a Kerrigan cousin inherited the old Keep. He found an old document describing the Kerrigan-O'Downey feud, which referred to the underground room. He hired a workman to remove the stones that sealed the door leading from the Great Hall to the room. He and several friends stood by as the door creaked on its one remaining hinge. A palpable chill crept from the rocky walls and seeped into their bones as they watched the workman feel his way down the long tunnel-like stairway, step by step.

Michael peered over the edge and saw the light of the workman's torch far below. It was extinguished with a shout and a barrage of stones. When the man stumbled back up the stairs, his body was imprinted with bloody handprints and the imprint of large flat stones. The workman died without speaking again. A year later, Michael Dartry died in a devastating fire in the living quarters of the castle.

In 1802, Fitz-Allen Dartry inherited the Keep. Rather than living in the grim old building, he designed a charming house, known as Kerrigan's Acre, about a mile away. There he entertained guests and enjoyed fox hunting. A dashing Coldstream Guard officer called Hambleton came to visit. After hearing the stories about the Keep, he declared that he must descend the fatal stairs into the hidden room.

Fitz-Allen said, "Absolutely not."

"Don't be silly, old man. Of course, I must face these demons from the past."

"But I would hold myself accountable if anything were to happen."

The only thing that's going to happen is that you will be toasting me in fine champagne in about sixty minutes."

Soon six men gathered in the Great Hall. Two laborers used crowbars to pry open the door into the graveyard room. The other side of the door was black with an odd fungus. They could feel the chill coming up the stairs, and the smell of rot and mold was a cold breath from deep within the keep. Beneath it seemed to lie an even more noxious odor, which was so bad that the onlookers covered their noses against this decay of ages. Hambleton lit a match, and the group saw a narrow tunnel stretching ahead onto a steeply slanting flight of stairs leading down into darkness. The match guttered, and he let it drop. Holding a handkerchief to his nose and lighting a pit lamp, Hambleton turned and waved happily to his friends. "I'll put an end to all these stories of feudal vengeance and supernatural phenomena. You will be praising me quite soon."

For a few minutes, all was quiet. Then, those waiting heard shouting and a barrage of stones. It ended as quickly as it began. When all was silent, they ran to the stairs and saw a badly beaten Hambleton lying halfway up the stairs.

Hambleton lived for ten days after this experience, although nearly every bone in his body was broken and he was covered with huge purple bruises. He said, "As I started down the stairs, I saw what appeared to be the stones in the floor heaving, undulating rather like a swell in the ocean. I tried to call out, but I had lost my voice. The stones seemed to rise up on end and everywhere I saw eyes staring at me. Great skeleton hands with rags still clinging to the bones lifted from the ground. Each hand held a flat stone dripping with blood. As the cries became louder, the hands hurled their stones at me."

After Hambleton died, the room was sealed again. The stories about the infamous stone room and its horrors continued, but there hasn't been any recurrence since Hambleton. The room was sealed, and a subsequent fire made the castle unlivable.

In 1924, an exorcist, named Dr. Santly, claiming to expel all ghosts came to visit Mrs. Tancred Kerrigan-Dartry in Kerrigan's Acre. Dr. Santly wanted to visit the Graveyard Room. He nagged and nagged. Finally, Mrs. Kerrigan-Dartry agreed. A workman removed four or five stones so the doctor could crawl through on his hands and knees. As the workman sat in the Great Hall waiting for the doctor to emerge, he heard a low roar and then stones hitting stones. The doctor came rushing up the stairs and tried to leap over the cliffs where the workman caught him. Shortly afterwards, he was committed to a retreat house for the hopelessly insane, Asylum of St. John of God's near Dublin.

The door to the Graveyard Room was sealed again, and the old keep was left to fall into complete ruin.

A late thirteenth century hall-house, Annaghkeen Castle in County Galway, is thought to be Ireland's oldest example of a castle built entirely from undressed stone. The Norman DeBurgo family built it and the nearby Cargin Castle to defend the Manor of Headford from incursions across Lough Corrib by the rival O'Flaherty clan. Their long-running feud with the O'Flaherty clan stems from the DeBurgos' arrival in Galway, when they took the O'Flaherty's lands and then tried to lease the land back to them. When no rent was paid, one of the DeBurgo clan was sent to the O'Flaherty stronghold at Aughanure Castle in Oughterard to collect payment. When he arrived at the castle, the O'Flahertys were feasting, and he was invited to join them. During the banquet, the DeBurgo man mentioned the missing rent, at which point an O'Flaherty pressed down on a concealed flagstone that hurled the man into the river. Living up to their name as the "Ferocious O'Flaherties," they then cut off his head and sent it back to the remaining DeBurgos, describing it as "O'Flaherty's rent." *Courtesy of Ciaran McHugh.*

The Wizard

When Henry VIII executed his older brother, Silken Thomas, and his five uncles in the Tower of London in 1537 and confiscated the Fitzgerald lands for rebellion, young Gerald Fitzgerald was the only family survivor. Smuggled to Tuscany, Gerald became fascinated with the black arts. Many of the professors at his esteemed university were quick to express their opinions on astronomy and necromancy; consequently, many of their students, along with Gerald, began thinking differently about the heavens and magic.

In 1552, Gerald was restored to his ancestral title and possessions. When he returned home, people noticed that even in sunlight he cast no shadow. Crows followed him everywhere, and one perched faithfully on his shoulder. The villagers called him a wizard. He laughed and went to his tower room where he worked on his magic.

Gerald married a beautiful young woman, who doted on him. She wanted to know everything about him, and he was happy to share his life with her, given that he had no other family. They spent a lot of time together, laughing, talking, and playing. They both knew how lucky they were that their marriage was one of love – not just an organized arrangement, which was common in those days. She made a great wife, ordering the servants, laughing at his jokes, and listening to his stories. There was only one thing that made her unhappy; he adamantly refused to take her into the locked room in the tower where he would disappear for hours. She even tried to get into it on her own when he was off settling a dispute with their neighbors, but the door was locked tight.

"Please, my dear, " she would beg, running her hands, up and down his back, "If you love me, you would show me what it is that you do up there."

"I cannot show you, my love," he would reply, kissing her briskly.

"Perhaps you are like Bluebeard and keep some monstrous secret hidden up there," she teased.

"You must not enter that room under any circumstances," he warned.

"But why do you feel this way, my dear. You are no Bluebeard." She would wrap her arms around him, electrifying him with her touch. "Please, I'll do anything you want. You know I can't resist you."

Finally, he succumbed. "Well if you really want to go up to my dirty tower room…"

"Oh, but I do."

"You will be bored."

"Never. If it makes you happy, I want to understand it."

"Well, you must not say a word – no matter what happens. Otherwise, I will be cursed."

"Well, I would not be a fit wife for you, if I were easily frightened. You do this for me, and you'll see how strong I am!"

Up they went, climbing the stairs in single file. The walls were rough dark stone, cold to the touch. The light of Gerald's torch was before them, and their shadows marched beside them on the walls. Behind them was blackness. When they reached the drafty tower room, she sat quietly, ignoring the crows nestled near the lofty ceiling. Gerald transformed himself to a giant bird with huge sharp beak, and claws. Then he became a ferocious dog who stood almost five feet high and bared his teeth growling. The dog slowly approached the countess, where he stood nose to nose with her. True to her promise, she said nothing, although she did back up a little. A large sea serpent that writhed across the floor, lashing his tail at her feet replaced the dog. Finally, Gerald returned to his human form, but his body was stretched so long that his head touched the ceiling and his feet the floor. At that, his wife screamed and fainted.

When she revived, Gerald was gone forever.

The only sign of him since that day is that, every seven years, his ghost is said to rise from the lake and ride across its surface on his great black horse who is shod with silver hooves. The curse on the Earl is said to be that he must ride these waters once every seven years until he has worn the silver on the hooves entirely away.

As for his curious wife, she never saw her beloved husband again.

Deserted houses , such as the Easkey ruin in County Sligo, abound in Ireland. Their doors bang in the wind, spiders and small animals scuttle about, and rumors spread about the strange shadows at night. *Courtesy of Ciaran McHugh.*

THE SHORT LIFE OF COLUM BLANEY

Irish history has many bloodstained tales of horror. Perhaps that's why there are so many ghosts. James Reynolds in *More Ghosts in Irish Houses* tells a tale of a brutal barbarous man.

Many nobles used to give room and board to the young sons of other nobles for several years so they could improve their manners and ability to deal in the world. Many boys profited by this arrangement, but Colum Blaney, who was sent to the massively built Bragheehooly Castle in County Offaly, had a hard road ahead. The castle's chieftain, Rone O'Hooley, was a brutal man: dark in hair and skin and dark in character. He only liked fighting and hunting, and they say that was because he loved blood.

O'Hooley had routed the enemy and was home to celebrate in his castle. Two men-at-arms, stood in front of an archway curtained with deer hides and furs to greet the celebrants. The wine flowed in the immense hall, which was drafty despite the enormous fire built from eight-foot logs roaring in a great hearth. The courses came and went: a thick soup of barley and venison, periwinkles fresh from the sea, and pigeon pie.

O'Hooley nodded at the group assembled before him. He held up his goblet of wine and took a long, thirsty sip, as if he had drunk nothing before that day. "Let's celebrate our win. It's the beginning of the new era." Everyone drank and O'Hooley slammed down his goblet. "Now, more food." Course after course appeared, borne by the pages on large trays. O'Hooley's fingers shone with oil; grease dripped from his mouth.

The noise of the crowd grew louder with each course. Finally, the pages began to serve the wild boars, which had been roasting for hours, turning slowly on wooden spits while kitchen boys basted them with butter and herbs. Feet stamped with anticipation. Mugs clanged against the wooden boards of the table.

Unfortunately, 14-year-old Colum Blaney, who was in attendance on O'Hooley, tripped over a wolfhound scavenging scraps of food lying among the rushes spread ankle-deep on the stones of the banquet floor. Colum fell, spilling his immense cauldron of steaming hot wild boar laced with an oily sauce on O'Hooley's chest and face. O'Hooley bellowed in agony. The murmuring, chatting, and clanging halted. Colum scrambled up from the floor where he had landed and ran down the hall toward the archway. Shouting with rage, O'Hooley rose to his feet, hot grease dripping from his bushy eyebrows. The silence grew until it was unbearable. O'Hooley grasped the knife lying on the table in front of him and hurled it at the fleeing Colum. The knife sped through the air, piercing Colum's neck just under one ear. It sank to the hilt, the steel protruding from the other side of his throat. A woman screamed, and O'Hooley turned, "Have you forgotten who I am? Be silent."

Colum fell senseless to the floor, bleeding profusely. One woman started to rise to go to the dying boy when O'Hooley with boar juices dripping from his face bellowed, "Leave him alone. I'm not finished yet." He strode down the hall, where he stooped and hoisted the still breathing boy over his shoulder.

The hall was totally silent, but no one made a move to interfere as Rone O'Hooley with his bleeding moaning burden strode over to the enormous crackling fireplace. Standing in front of the fire, O'Hooley addressed the silent hall, "When I throw something, I'm always straight to the mark." At that, he picked up Colum's body by the feet, swung his body around his head, and then dumped it into the writhing flames. The crowded hall gasped as the flames grew brighter and the boy's yellow hair crackled in the flames. Those who attended would never forget this celebration.

To this day, a young boy running for his life haunts the castle.

Werewolves of Ossory

When I was a little girl, my grandmother, who was Irish, used to tell me all sorts of stories. I can remember sitting on her big, comfortable lap and she would tell me stories about witches, leprechauns, banshees, and the occasional werewolf. It wasn't until I was a teenager that I learned about the werewolves of Ossory, who were half men, half wolves that roamed the forest areas of Ireland. I had several nightmares after hearing the story.

Many years ago, she told me, a priest and a young novice from one of the Ulster religious houses had to travel through the Irish forests to Meath. These were the times when people feared the Devil and were worried that they might meet the Evil One on the road. The priest felt himself to have been fortunate not to have met him on this long wearisome journey. He and the boy walked alone, accompanied by the chirrup of birds, the stirrings of the forest, and the occasional unmistakable howling of wolves. Night was not far away, and strange shapes and shadows were flitting across the forest track in the final rays of the sun. Since night was coming, they looked for a safe spot to sleep, but all they saw was an empty trail shadowed by monstrous trees. The forest was growing darker and the evening shadows longer as they found a small cave, and the priest told the novice to gather twigs and dried moss to start a fire. Meanwhile, he used his knife to cut branches from nearby bushes to add to it. Then the priest told the novice to catch a rabbit. Amazingly enough, he did. They sighed with relief. They had a fire to keep away the wild animals and meat for supper. They skewered and cooked the rabbit, said Grace, ate their meal of rabbit and oaten bread, said their prayers, pulled their bags underneath them, and fell asleep as the fire slowly burned and the forest surrounded them with its evening, *chirp-chirp* choral music.

The priest woke up in the middle of the night. He knew something had awakened him, but he didn't know what it was until he realized that the woods were silent. Totally silent. Then he heard something large moving through the forest. Leaves rustled, a branch snapped, and the priest knew he was dealing with a predator in the dark. In a gap, he saw two baleful eyes glaring from a dim crouching shape. The priest grabbed a branch from the fire and waved it around him like a torch. "Wake up, wake up," he whispered to the sleeping novice. "We may have trouble." The novice rolled over.

"Who's there?" the priest asked, grasping the crucifix that hung about his neck, for he was afraid of things that lurked in the night. Perhaps it was the Devil.

"I will not harm you, priest," said a harsh voice.

"How do you know I am a priest?"

"I know."

The priest held out his crucifix in front of him. He knew that the Devil was the father of all lies and that this might be a trick to lure him and the boy into the darkness. "What can I do for you?"

"I am a repentant sinner who wants you to grant me and my wife absolution for our sins," rasped the voice.

"If that is so, step forward into the light of my fire and reveal yourself to me."

"I am afraid to. For you will find my appearance to be unlike anything you have seen."

"My son, I have seen many things in my forty years. I have seen people maimed and killed and people suffering from many diseases, and I have always given them my blessing. I doubt that you can alarm me or disgust me."

The boy had awakened by this time and was staring wide-eyed into the forest. Beyond the firelight, something large moved, and a huge slavering grey wolf with red lantern eyes and long canine teeth approached the small area near the fire.

"There," said the wolf. "This is who I am. I bet that your boy is terrified." He stretched and pawed at the ground. The priest shook his head, backing away quickly from the enormous creature with the long, sharp teeth.

"What do you want?" asked the priest. The creature resembled a wolf, but what wolf balanced easily on its hind legs? This had to be a creature of the devil.

"Once I was like you – a human who walked on two feet – but my clan and I were cursed by the Abbot Natalis for some long-forgotten sin. Every seven years two of us become wolves, living in the forest."

"You're telling me you are a human?"

"Yes, and we are still devout Christians in need of help and blessing."

The priest sighed. "Do you mean that although you look like a wolf, you worship God?"

"That's true," agreed the wolf. "Although we appear to be wolves, we are humans who sin and who wish forgiveness."

The priest pondered the wolf's words. After all, wolves didn't speak with human voices, and this one certainly did. "And why did the Abbot curse you?"

"For a long-forgotten sin by my forefathers," said the wolf, "but the curse is still in force because he died before lifting it."

The listening boy nodded. Even at his young age, he knew that a curse remained unless the person who had originally placed the curse removed it.

The wolf drew closer. "It's hard to be a wolf when we are human. There is no wilderness to hide in. We can't run in packs in the forests because there aren't many forests to hide in. Now, the humans outnumber us, and we must live beside them. Not an easy thing to do.

"My wife and I were old when we became wolves more that six years ago. Recently, some hunters spotted my wife and shot her. She was wounded badly and is dying as we speak. She wants to confess her sins and have absolution before she dies."

"And you want me to come with you and administer the final sacraments to her?" The wolf nodded.

"I will," said the priest for he was a kind-hearted man who had been moved by the wolf's story. "Boy, you stay here and keep the fire well lit so I can find my way back," he said, motioning to the boy to remain where he was by the fire. Grabbing a branch from the fire to use as a torch, and holding his crucifix tight, the priest followed the wolf into the dark woods. Every shadow seemed darker, every sound more ominous. The trees pressed close and shut out the light of the swollen moon.

The wolf moved swiftly and silently ahead of the old man, who blundered through the undergrowth, branches scraping him as he worked hard to negotiate the forest path. When the wind set the leaves to rustling, it was like a chilly finger up his spine. The moon was sinking below the trees when they reached their destination: a fork in the trail, marked by a huge tree hung over a small stream. In a small cave among the jumbled roots lay an old she-wolf, with a deep puncture wound in her chest. At their approach, she raised her tired head.

"My dear wife," said the first wolf in a low and soothing voice. "I have succeeded and brought a priest to give you the final sacraments."

The old priest knelt down next to the dying she-wolf. "Who are you?" he whispered. Blood seeped down her fur from her wound and from between her teeth.

"My husband probably told you already," she answered. "We are the Werewolves of Ossory, condemned to live as wolves for a long ago crime. Hunters attacked us, and one wounded me. I want to confess my sins before I die. Will you grant me your blessing, Father?"

The priest nodded hesitantly.

"You think we are evil," she said. "You think that this is some trick of the Evil One?"

The priest nodded again.

"But you are wrong. Underneath my pelt, I'm as human and as Christian as yourself."

The priest still seemed uncertain.

"What will it take to convince you?" asked the male wolf, rearing up on its hind-legs. "You're a priest. I can't bribe you. What can I do? If I were to walk like a man would that convince you that we are truly human?"

The priest licked his dry lips uneasily. "You say that you are human, but I just see two wolves. And certainly you speak like humans, but your words come through a mouth with razor-sharp teeth. If...if I could but see the human that you say lurks beneath the wolf-skin, then my mind would be at rest."

Eyes glazed with exhaustion, the female wolf straightened herself painfully. The priest drew back in alarm but then saw that she did not mean to threaten him.

"I will show you my true face." She brought her right forepaw to her jaws and began to gnaw at the skin. Blood spurted and part of the leg fell away to reveal the fingers of a human hand below. Raising the hand to its belly, the female wolf proceeded to rip and tear at the flesh there, pulling it back and opening it as though it were a hairy garment. The wolf-head seemed to fall away like a mask, leaving an old woman, wrinkled and exhausted.

The priest crossed himself. The woman's ancient mouth worked to form words. "There, you see for yourself, Father. Now do you believe?"

He nodded in amazement.

"Now, Father," said the male wolf. "You know our story. You know that we are human and are true believers. Will you hear my wife's confession and give her last rites?"

The priest sighed. *Sometimes,* he thought, *those who call themselves Christian are far worse in their ways than the pagans.*

"Of course, I will hear your confession," he said sadly. He knelt down next to the old woman to hear her final confession. Then he reached within his robes for the small vial of oil that he carried to anoint her. He made the sign of the cross above her.

"I grant you my absolution," he said. "Go to meet your maker in peace."

The old woman leaned back as blood trickled from the corner of her mouth.

"Although my body dies in its present form," she whispered, "my immortal soul shall be with God." And she laid her head down and shut her eyes. That morning she was dead, and the male wolf threw back his head and howled. He pointed out the direction to the priest and went back to the dark woodland depths. Sadly, the priest turned and continued on his journey.

His business in Meath took the priest much longer than he had expected and so it was early in the following year before he journeyed back to Ulster. On his way, he stopped in the woods of Ossory but, although he searched, he could not find any sign of the big male wolf at all. Perhaps hunters had killed him or maybe he had moved on. Either way there was not a trace of him to be seen, but as the sun was setting and the moon was riding high, the old priest heard a wolf howling at the moon.

Many ruins of churches can be found throughout Ireland. Ghosts may haunt some; others just may have sheep grazing! *Courtesy of Ciaran McHugh.*

The Vampire Sheriff

Carrickphouka* means *the rock of the phouka*; the phouka or pooka is a shape-shifter. Sometimes it appears as a great horse, sometimes as a feral goat with long curling horns. Sometimes it is benign; other times it is a malevolent demon.

Carrickphouka Castle, which means "Castle on the Rock of the Fairy" or "Castle on the Rock of the Phouka" (an Irish word for ghost or spirit), is perched high on an outcrop of rock overlooking the Sullane River in County Cork. Many people believe that Carrigaphooca is one of the most haunted castles in Ireland, and several phoukas are said to be linked to the castle. *Courtesy of Ciaran McHugh.*

The rock on which Carrickphouka Castle stood was supposed to be inhabited by one such devilish being.

In the mid-sixteenth century, the Tudor and Stuart monarchs began to uproot Irish landowners and establish Protestant settlements in Ireland. The early plantations tended to be based on small "exemplary" colonies. The later plantations were based on mass confiscations of land from Irish landowners and the subsequent importation of large numbers of settlers from England, Wales, and Scotland. The English authorities hoped that the colonists would act as a bulwark against further rebellions from the native Irish Catholics. They called this policy the Plantation policy. Naturally, the Irish considered this policy intolerable and relentlessly attacked the settlers.

In the Irish Midlands, the English appointed Cormac Tadhg McCarthy of Carrickphouka Castle the High Sheriff of Cork. Bone thin and bone hard, he had a fierce brooding face that might have been chipped from stone. His mission was to ruthlessly hunt down all Irish rebels.

The region seethed with hostility and bad blood. One of the leaders of the Irish rebels was James Fitzgerald, who had rallied a substantial band of dissatisfied Irish lords to descend upon the English settlers to rob and kill and melt away like snow whenever the English rode out in search of them. The situation was untenable. Cormac approached him and suggested that they make peace over a feast at his castle.

When Fitzgerald and his men entered the Great Hall of the castle, he could smell the meat, which had been roasting for hours, turning slowly on wooden spits, while kitchen boys basted it with butter and herbs until the meat crackled and spit. Such a smell was nectar to the Irish rebels who had been hiding in the forest for several weeks. The tables were piled high with fresh-baked bread, cheese, and strawberries. Fitzgerald was given a place of high honor to the left of the High Sheriff. The English lords sat on his right. Fitzgerald raised his hand to summon servants with flagons of wine and leaned over and filled Fitzgerald's cup himself.

In the middle of the lavish banquet, Cormac stood, pounding his cup on the table for attention. When the hubbub quieted, he bellowed, "Now." His men seized and killed Fitzgerald. The slaughter of Fitzgerald was a terrible way to abuse the Irish code of hospitality, but Cormac wanted to go one step further. He wanted to ensure the English of his loyalty and to impress them with his services. So once Fitzgerald was truly dead, he did an awful deed: he drank James Fitzgerald's blood and ate his flesh as everyone watched. The English were not impressed; they were disgusted.

In defense of Cormac's heinous actions, the McCarthy clan claimed that the evil spirit of the phouka had possessed Cormac, rising out of the rock upon which his castle was built. The castle was destroyed in 1690-91, but villagers still avoid its site. Some even genuflect for protection – even in broad daylight! At night, eerie screaming can be heard and the rocks around the castle ruins weep blood.

* Spellings seen for the castle include both *Carrickphouka* and *Carrigaphooca*.

Many believe that gates, like bridges, are a means to travel to another world. These gates posed as sentries to the Glen at Knocknarea, for probably more than two centuries. W. B. Yeats wrote about them in "The Man And The Echo":

In a cleft that's christened Alt
Under broken stone I halt
At the bottom of a pit
That broad noon has never lit,
And shout a secret to the stone.

Unfortunately, the gates were stolen in July 2011. *Courtesy of Ciaran McHugh.*

Malahide Castle Hauntings

Dating back to the twelfth century, Malahide Castle was originally a Norman Tower House. Today, it is a square, castellated building with circular towers flanking the corners. The old moat has been drained but not completely filled. The estate began in 1185, when Richard Talbot, a knight who accompanied Henry II to Ireland in 1174, was granted the "lands and Harbour of Malahide." It was home to the Talbot family, from 1185 until 1976. The only period when it didn't belong to them was under Cromwell, who granted it to Miles Corbet from 1649-1660. Once Cromwell died, Corbet was hanged, and the Talbots regained their castle.

According to the legend, during Corbet's occupancy, the figure of the Virgin, which represented the ascent of the Coronation of the Virgin, vanished from the carved chimney piece in the Oak Room of the castle. Once Cromwell died and Charles II ascended the throne, the Virgin miraculously resumed her place in the sculptured setting. There she can be seen today.

The same Miles Corbet, who was hung once Cromwell had died, is associated with another of the castle's ghostly stories. Corbet was one of the signatories to the death warrant of King Charles I. He is said to have suffered from insomnia while living at Malahide, and his conscience forced him to spend his sleepless nights riding a grey horse around the castle grounds. Many believe that the horse is the much-feared Phouka, which is always out after the sun sets, creating harm and mischief. Local tradition claims that the area known as the Back Ghost Road today was once known as Corbet's Ride. Every year on the anniversary of his death, onlookers can hear, if not see, Corbet on his galloping Phouka.

For nearly 800 years, the Talbot family lived in the Castle. They saw many changes, many births and deaths. During the Battle of the Boyne in 1690, when William III vanquished James II and his army, fourteen members of the Talbot family are said to have sat down to breakfast in the Great Hall that July morning, and the same fourteen were all dead by that evening.

Various Ladies

For many years, the painting of a very beautiful anonymous lady, in a flowing white dress, hung in the Great Hall of Malahide. Nobody appeared to know her identity or the identity of the artist who portrayed her. It had been recorded that from time to time she would leave her painting and wander through the castle in the quiet of the night. She has become known as the White Lady.

In the castle grounds is a field called Our Lady's Acre, which is also said to have some meandering ghosts. On a few occasions, two grey-haired, sad-faced ladies have been seen, wandering aimlessly. Nobody knows the reasons for their sojourn. Some sources suggest that they are ghosts of Danish women who never found rest once the Norman Talbot drove the Danes from the area.

THE RESIDENT JESTER CARETAKER

Given its age, Malahide Castle has its fair share of ghostly traditions. Aat one time, a man named Puck was the resident caretaker. Four foot tall and bearded, he was responsible for keeping watch and sounding the alarm in case of attack. He lived in a turret of the castle, now known as Puck's Staircase, where he carried out his duties as watchman in the most dedicated manner. Some say that Puck fell in love with a noblewoman from Lady Elenora Fitzgerald's retinue. Ultimately, he hanged himself from the Minstrel's Gallery, overlooking the Great Hall.

He may have died, but he is not gone, according to the Talbot family history. He has been seen in photographs taken in the Great Hall. His wrinkled, impish face has appeared through the ivy covering his turret.

Before the castle was open to the public, an occasional guided tour used to take place. On nearing the area of Puck's Staircase, the guide always used to ask her visitors to "please, stand aside; make way for Puck." His last appearance was in 1976, when he appeared before the sale of Malahide Castle's contents. A member of Sotheby's staff was sitting in the Great Hall itemizing material for the pending auction, when he swears that Puck appeared on his staircase. Without any prior knowledge, the staff member described Puck as he had been known to generations of Talbots. Puck did approve of the sale.

BLOODY BRIDGE

Simmering with bitterness at the English who had stripped them of their position and property, the Irish clans would retreat to the hills and bogs and carry on guerilla warfare against the English settlers. The English would subdue them by force, which resulted in further dispossession of rebels' lands as punishment. Ultimately, the festering hatred of the native population for colonists exploded into warfare.

In October 1641, the Irish, who had lost their homes and lands, attacked the English and Scottish Protestant settlers who had arrived in the Ulster Plantation about thirty years earlier. At first, the settlers were beaten and robbed; later their houses were burned; then they were expelled from the area. Farms and straggling villages lay ruined, roofless, if they stood at all. Old and young, Protestant men, women, and children perished by the edge of the road from exposure, hunger, and disease. By November 1641, as winter began to set in, armed parties of Ulstermen were rounding up British settlers and marching them to the coast. There, the Irish forced them to board ships to Britain.

In what is now called Portadown, County Armagh, the Irish imprisoned one group of English Protestants, consisting of many women and children, in a church. After some time, the English civilians were removed from the church and marched to a wooden bridge over the River Bann. On the way, they were robbed and stripped of their valuables and most or all of their clothes. Once on the bridge, the Irish halted the group. The rebels threatened their captives with pikes and swords and left them shivering naked on that raw November day. The Irish captors then heaped brushwood and kindling on each end of the bridge and ignited the old wooden bridge. The only way the civilians could escape was by jumping into the chilly river flowing swiftly underneath them. When they jumped off the bridge to flee the fire, the Irish shot them down – even the women with infants in arms. Soon the bridge was burning furiously. Everyone perished either by flames or smoke or water. Those who tried to swim to shore were driven back into the water with long pikes where they died.

There were witnesses who testified to the incident. Supposedly, the river ran red with blood for weeks, and there was a massive fish kill in a river that usually teemed with salmon. Since then, bobbing human heads crying and moaning have been seen in the water. In the space once spanned by the bridge, a woman and baby are seen exhorting the British government to avenge their deaths. Sometimes the woman simply appears to be crying over the dead. Anger can still be found flowing along with the river.

Bridges are often said to be haunted. Perhaps it is because they are often associated with the dead crossing the bridge to reach the afterlife. Some believe bridges are haunted because they cover running water that acts as a magnet for supernatural occurrences. *Courtesy of Ciaran McHugh.*

The Ghosts of Ross Castle

In the late fifteenth century, the English controlled the pale, an area extending west from Dublin to the shores of Lough Sheelin. Beyond this area, the Irish chieftains and their clans reigned. At the edge of the pale were the Nugent lands. Their forefather had received the land and titles in payment for participating in William the Conqueror's 1066 invasion of England. The family was loyal to the Crown and did its utmost to maintain, and where possible, expand their foothold in the new colony. When the English Crown granted the extensive sum of ten pounds sterling for every fortification or tower house erected by their subjects in Ireland, Richard Nugent, the twelfth Baron of Delvin, began to build Ross Castle at the top of a steep hill on the shores of Lough Sheelin, overlooking the enemy territory of the O'Reillys to the north. Stone from the nearby Ross quarry was used to erect the formidable tower, the walled living quarters, and defensive buildings.

The Black Baron

Richard Nugent, called the Black Baron, was a mean-tempered man, quick to anger, slow to forgive. He had a neck and shoulders like a bull and an ugly scar down one side of his face. People still tell about the day that a town's woman had just finished baking her bread and placed a large loaf on the windowsill of her cottage to cool when a dog happened to come down the narrow path and smell that fresh bread. The dog grabbed the bread and ran. No sooner had this happened, than the woman realized that the dog had taken the loaf and yelled "Thief! Thief!" The dog dropped the bread and ran for cover. Meanwhile, the Black Baron and his followers were hunting when he heard about the stolen bread. Infuriated by the lawlessness in his realm, he stormed and raged.

Not much later, a beggar passed through the village. He decided to take a nap under a tree. Of course, the Baron soon met the sleeping beggar, who he shook awake. In his eyes, the beggar had taken the bread. The beggar fell to his knees, pleading his innocence. "Noble sir, I know nothing about any bread. I just fell asleep."

"You are a liar," the Baron shouted. "I won't have liars and thieves in my village. String him up." The Baron's men obediently hung the beggar. After all, one didn't quarrel with Richard Nugent, the Black Baron, the master of his land and people.

Later, the townspeople found the missing bread. They planted a cross at the place where the beggar's makeshift gallows stood. Five hundred years later, the story of the Baron's cruelty is still remembered.

SABRINA

The Black Baron had a beautiful daughter, Sabrina. She reached womanhood having most of her desires quickly gratified by her proud father. Some would say she was spoiled. But she had a smile that could steal your heart and eyes as blue as the skies on a warm summer's day, and unlike her father, she was always nice to the village folk.

One day she was walking down to the bridge across the River Inny, which formed the border of her father's dominion, when she met a handsome young man. Son of an O'Reilly chieftain, his name was Orvin. As always in stories of this type, the two young people, one the daughter of an English lord and the other the son of an Irish chieftain, took one look at each other and their hearts were forsworn for eternity. The trees swayed and sighed with them, the air was warm on their faces, and they were in love. Knowing that their fathers would be dismayed, they met in secret, concealing their passion for each other from the public.

They met on the mountaintops, in the forests, and in the valleys. They whispered tender words and promises to each other; they laughed with wonder and joy as they stared into each other's eyes. Every day they met, and every day they were a little bolder with each other. He would take her hands in his and lift them to his lips, kissing each finger. When their fingers touched, she could feel an odd exhilarating shiver run through her body; his breath stirred her hair...and she felt herself melting.

One day, they decided to elope and find their fortune elsewhere. One night, they met secretly at Lough Sheelin, where they boarded a boat down by the shore and started to row across the lake. As they were on their way, the winds began to blow from the west. The wind got stronger, as did the waves. A sudden swell caught the boat and overturned it. Sabrina survived but Orwin drowned. Upon realizing that he was dead, Sabrina became deeply depressed. She stopped eating and drinking and finally died.

To this day, Sabrina haunts the castle's walls. The villagers say her father's banishment of Orvin and other cruel deeds caused Sabrina's unhappiness and eventual death. Visitors have often met her ghost, still in search for her lover and restless until the day she will be reunited with him. Others have reported the Black Baron's presence; some have seen faces in wardrobes, and men sitting at the foot of their beds in the dead of night. Mediums have woken up covered in fresh scratches while others have detected musky smells and heard church bells ringing out and pianos playing.

The Irish had a prophecy that Ross Castle would never be taken until a warship could swim on the lake. During the Irish Confederate Wars, Oliver Cromwell's Roundheads brought the artillery in by boat via the River Laune. The sight of the ships unnerved the defenders, who soon surrendered.

The castle is said to be the ancestral home of the O'Donoghue clan. One legend says O'Donoghue leaped, or was sucked out, of the window of the grand chamber at the top of the castle and disappeared into the waters of the lake along with his horse, his table, and his library. Supposedly, O'Donoghue now lives in a great palace at the bottom of the lake, where he keeps a close eye on everything that he sees. *Courtesy of Ciaran McHugh*

Grace O'Malley and the Rat

"Riverrun, past Eve and Adam's, from swerve of shore to bend of bay, brings us by a commodius vicus of recirculation back to Howth Castle and Environs."

—The opening sentence of
James Joyce's *Finnegans Wake*
giving directions to Howth Castle.

Howth Castle

In 1593, after many difficult years fighting against the English and the capture of her brother and son by English forces, the sixteenth century Irish pirate, Grace O'Malley, visited Queen Elizabeth to make peace and ask for the release of her brother and son. As she returned from this visit, Grace landed at Howth and proceeded to the castle, hoping to be admitted to dine with Lord Howth and to obtain supplies for her voyage back to Mayo. The gates of the castle were closed to her, which she considered to be against the ancient Irish tradition of hospitality.

In revenge, she abducted the Earl's grandson and heir and took him to Clew Bay. She returned him when his family promised that they would never close the gates at dinner hour and a place would always be laid at table for the unexpected guest. Lord Howth gave her a ring as pledge on the agreement. The ring remains in the possession of Grace's descendant, and to this day the extra place is laid at Howth Castle. In the town of Howth, a Grace O'Malley Road commemorates these events.

The Shipwrecked Woman

Several decades later, a large storm came to Howth Bay. Thunder boomed, rolling slowly across the horizon and then echoing back again. The clouds twisted and rolled, now black, then purple, and then gradually spreading over the entire sky. High waves rolled in, sending spume over the cliffs. Far out in the bay, a ship rocked crazily in the pounding waves and then foundered under the lowering black sky. The cries and screams of the people still on board carried across the bay as the hulk shuddered and rolled. That morning jagged splinters of wood, half-submerged barrels, deck chairs, a child's doll, bodies, and a lovely young woman were found on the beach. The woman's body was draped lifelessly across a wooden plank, and her silvery blond hair fanned out around her head on the sand. Found to be breathing, she was brought to the castle where the women of the castle cared for her.

When the Earl of Howth visited her bedside, she told him her name was Genevieve and that her family had been on the ship. Now, she was alone in the world at age 17. He was struck by her beauty and tragic story. Once she had recovered from her ordeal, he pressed her to stay on in the castle. Her haunting eyes were lit with intelligence, and her shape delightfully feminine.

"Do you ride?" he asked. "We can ride tomorrow."

"I do."

The next morning, a breeze blew steadily from the hills. Canopies of white clouds threw cool shadows over the great lawns. He found himself looking for Genevieve and ignoring his friends. Half way through the ride, she murmured her excuses and disappeared into the wood. The Earl went after her. He found her in a rocky glen, sitting on a large fallen tree. Her hair was in curly disorder around her slender neck. He sat down beside her.

A bird trilled a long high note.

She reached out and touched his cheekbones lightly as if she were wiping away a speck of dirt. His throat hurt.

He wished the two of them could stay frozen in this moment. He let his fingertips move across her mouth for a long second. "Meet me tomorrow," he said.

"Where?"

They began riding every day. She had a sexy, throaty voice, which he loved. Of course, people found out. His intended fiancé, Alice, stomped her foot and walked away when he entered a room. The Earl didn't care as long as Genevieve was there. She made him laugh. No one had ever made him laugh.

His family was aghast. They forbid him to see her. He was destroying their plans for the future. "You must not do this. A union with an unknown shipwrecked victim without any family doesn't help us."

He didn't care. He was madly in love with her – the kind of love that comes only once in a lifetime, he announced. Although he pressured Genevieve to marry him, she refused not once, but several times. She told him that it was impossible, that they came from different worlds. Then she gave him a ribbon woven with strange words and signs, told him to wear it always on his wrist, and she disappeared.

Eventually, he gave in to his family's demands and married Alice, who was from a nearby family with excellent connections.

Alice was Genevieve's opposite. She rarely smiled and certainly didn't make him laugh. She kept the drapes pulled and the sunlight out, snapped at the servants, and kept all the dogs outside. He stared sadly at the ribbon he wore around his wrist and went hunting frequently.

When Alice realized that Genevieve had given him the ribbon, she was most annoyed. She nagged and begged, but he insisted on wearing it day and night.

"Once and for all, Alice," said he, "it's out of the question. I shall be gravely displeased if you return to this matter."

"Well," said Alice. "Now I know the esteem in which I am held." Then she began to cry.

Like most men, the Earl had a horror of a woman's sobs. "I made Genevieve a promise."

Alice sobbed even louder. "Here, I am your wife, and you are keeping a promise to another."

One night, she plied him with Irish whiskey. Once he fell asleep, snoring loudly, Alice quietly cut the ribbon off his wrist and dropped it into the fire. When he realized it was missing, she looked blankly at him. "What ribbon are you talking about?"

"I wouldn't put it past you to have taken it off. If you did, you have brought us bad luck." He didn't speak to her for the next week.

One night, the palace dogs chased a white rat into the Great Hall. The hunted rat jumped on the table right in front of Earl Howth. Something about that rat spoke to the Earl, and he stopped the dogs. "This rat needs me or I need her." From then on, despite the scorn of his wife and followers, he kept the rat with him. Often he carried it on his person. You can imagine how distressed his wife was. There she would be wearing her finery at a fancy ball, and her husband was stroking a rat!

The Earl talked to the rat frequently. The rat would watch him intently, while Alice stormed and screamed. Then the rat would shake and lean on the Earl's sleeve, looking soulfully into his eyes. One day, Alice had a servant trap the white rat, which she beat to death with a heavy poker in front of the Earl.

The Earl died that night, his brother inherited the estate, and Alice was left with nothing. Some say a white rat still haunts the castle.

One brother killed his brother, a priest, during a sacred mass at what is now known as the Bloody Chapel in Leap Castle in County Offaly. This castle is the source of many tales of evil spirits. *Courtesy of Ciaran McHugh.*

Raised in Blood: Leap Castle

Ireland was divided into a patchwork quilt of estates ruled by local lords. In the absence of a strong central authority, the rivalries among families and between family members could become intense. Many say that Ireland's most haunted castle is Leap Castle in Offaly with its violent and turbulent history. Its blood-drenched legend says that it was built in the early 1500s over an earlier castle on a site used by Druids for initiation ceremonies. Supposedly, an ancient curse hangs over it: "Raised in blood, blood be its portion."

Its builders, the O'Bannon clan, were the secondary chieftains under the ruling of the O'Carrolls, chieftains of the area. According to the storytellers, two O'Bannon brothers were contesting the chieftainship of their clan. The only way they could settle their argument was by a display of strength and bravery. They agreed that they would leap off the rocky outcrop where the castle was to be built. The survivor would be the Chieftain. Thus the castle built on blood and death was named Leim Ui Bhanainmeaning or "Leap of the O'Bannons."

The O'Carroll Clan

Leap Castle became the principal stronghold of the O'Carroll clan, a fierce and brutal people, bent on domination. They were known for their ruthless tactics, often killing others and each other on the path to supremacy. When the O'Carrolls seized the castle, they are said to have mixed the blood of the defeated O'Bannons with the mortar as they expanded the old fortress.

In 1532, when the O'Carroll chieftain died, One-Eyed Tadhg and Thaddeus O'Carroll, who were brothers, began to compete for the position of chieftain. A priest, Thaddeus, was holding mass for his family members when his rival, Tadhg, burst into the chapel, fatally wounding him. Thaddeus fell across the altar and died in front of his family. Many have seen his spirit in what is now known as the Bloody Chapel. His spirit has also been seen lurking on the stairway below and leaving the chapel via the western door to the bartizan and down the northern stairs. The murderous Tadhg was condemned to become a vampire ghost when he died for this blasphemous act.

But before he died, Tadhg added to the bloody legends about the castle. One night, he invited forty members of an enemy clan to a banquet under the guise of making peace. Supposedly, he then pushed them down the oubliette (a secret dungeon entered by a ceiling trap door) to land on a spike eight feet below. If they were not fortunate enough to die quickly on the spike, they died of starvation. Eventually, his cousin murdered him. A very bloody family.

In 1688, the O'Carrolls finally left Ireland in return for a grant from the English of 60,000 acres of land in America. The family played a major role in the state of Maryland, and one member even signed the Declaration of Independence. The New World was a happier place for them.

In the beginning of the twentieth century, workmen, hired to clean out the oubliette, uncovered a large pile of human skeletons. Supposedly, they needed three carts to remove all the bones. Among the bones, workmen found a pocket watch made in the 1840s. It is not certain if the dungeon was still in use then.

The Red Lady

The Bloody Chapel is the home to many Leap Castle ghosts. One is known as The Red Lady, who is a very tall woman clothed in a red dress. She has been seen carrying a dagger in her hand, raised in a menacing manner. A strange luminescence is seen radiating within her. People encountering this spirit have commented on an immense cold filling the room and permeating into their hearts. It is thought that the woman was captured by an O'Carroll and subsequently raped. O'Carroll killed the baby born from this violent act, saying he couldn't afford to feed it. Distraught, the woman then killed herself with the same blade.

In 1659, ownership of Leap Castle passed by marriage from the O'Carroll family to an English family, the Darbys. The Darby family turned Leap Castle into their family home, with improvements and additions and landscaped gardens. In the late nineteenth century, Jonathan and Mildred Darby were looking forward to living there. At that time, people were fascinated by the occult, and Mildred Darby dabbled in magic. She saw many different apparitions ranging from a monk with tonsure and cowl to a horrifying apparition, who induced an overwhelming sense of dread and deep-rooted fear. In an article, she described it as "a hideous looking thing with almost human-looking eyes and reeking of the most ghastly odor."

In 1922, Leap Castle became a target of the Irish struggle for independence and was burned. Completely gutted by fire, Leap Castle was boarded up, and its gates locked for over seventy years. While it was abandoned, locals described seeing the windows at the top of the castle "light up for a few seconds, as if many candles were brought into the room" late at night. The castle lay in ruins for years.

In the 1970s, it was bought. The new owner is said to have had a white witch brought in from Mexico to exorcise the castle. She spent many hours in the bloody chapel; when she emerged, she explained that the spirits at Leap Castle were no longer malevolent, but they wished to remain.

Temptation

Tall and darkly handsome, Andrew Rigby lived in one of Dublin's elegant old mansions. His family had come to Ireland when England established control over the Ulster region in northern Ireland. Once the native Irish were evicted from the region, loyal English and Scottish settlers were welcomed to the land on the condition they would keep the English ways and the Protestant religion. When Andrew's great-grandfather supported Cromwell, he was rewarded with more land for "Services rendered." Being rich gentry, Andrew's ancestors rarely lived in Ireland, but usually left their estates in the care of highly capable managers, who sublet the acreage to the Irish until the farming was done by the lowest tenant-farmer. After graduating from Oxford, Andrew went abroad to further his education in Paris and Florence, but then his newly widowed mother needed him back at home to oversee the Irish estate that had been suffering.

Yes, the impeccably tailored and groomed Andrew Rigby was an important man. In Dublin, his large fireplaced library replicated a room in an ancient French monastery and occupied the northeast wing of his mansion. In London, the walls of his house were covered with exquisite tapestries from Morocco and Spain. The pocket doors were massive, and the hardwood floors were stained dark. When he visited his estate in County Antrim, Andrew brought some of his household servants so he could maintain his style of living. He hired natives, who considered themselves fortunate to get the work carrying coal to the fireplaces, sweeping the dusty grates daily, loading the dumbwaiters, and mowing acres of lawns. He employed a laundress who starched his shirts and washed his mother's camisoles and petticoats, a kitchen maid who assisted the cook, a chambermaid who worked upstairs, and a parlor maid who worked downstairs. He was a much-envied man.

Andrew had business acquaintances and servants, but no one, other than his mother, who loved him. He had many beautiful women whom he escorted to the balls and parties, but no one excited him. He was frequently alone with his books, wondering if this was all that life offered. He had just about decided that it was when one evening as he was walking along the sea, he met a lovely dark-haired woman who had mocking eyes, and hair that smelled like the warm sun on an August meadow. She wore a gown as white as the foam on the waves and a bright scarlet cloak that stood out like a beacon. He thought her laughter was like sleigh bells on a crisp winter morning.

They walked and talked. She tucked her curls behind her ear and laughed up to him. The next morning he scanned the beach for her. There she stood on the sand like a fiery beacon. She saw him and waved. Andrew laughed. Women of his acquaintance didn't wave at a man. They waited for the man to come to them. He liked this woman and her passionate involvement with life. They walked along the beach, tossing shells into the surf. Her red cloak fluttered in the wind, her dark hair shone in the sun, and she threw back her head when she laughed.

He walked the beach the next morning and night – up and down, up and down, but she didn't appear in the next three days. The fourth day, she reappeared with a ghost of smile on her lips and her eyes alight with humor as if she were enjoying a private joke. He shared his lunch with her. They sat in a sheltered spot a few yards from the water. She wrapped her red cloak around her, laughing into the breeze, and took off her shoes. Andrew couldn't recall when he had last seen a woman's bare feet. Behind them was a crumbling cliff top. Before them birds rose and fell, riding the wind, scarcely moving their wings.

He was restless that night, tossing and turning, dreaming of dark glossy hair, red cloaks, and a laugh like sleigh bells.

Her clear-eyed gaze and her attention made him feel like a new man. He knew little about her background or where she came from, but he really didn't care. She did not appear to be governed by the etiquette rules that encumbered his friends' wives and their six wardrobe changes a day. When she came to Dublin to meet his mother and friends, she did all the right things, smiled frequently, and wore her red cloak. Sometimes he could hear her laugh from across the room. His friends adored her.

His mother did not. "She's Irish. Probably a Catholic," she snapped.

"That doesn't matter, Mother."

"You know nothing about her. Who's her family?"

He shrugged, and she continued.

"There are many tales of strange creatures living in the forest and hills here. Druids once lived in Ireland, you know."

But Andrew would have none of this. He had never known what it was like to find the perfect fit with another person, to be aroused by a simple passing contact. He was in love.

His mother continued. "Most women are more modest and refined. They don't wear bold red cloaks and meet men on beaches." He walked out of the room.

She made him feel so strong, so important, so valuable. One night, he knelt down in front of her and asked her to marry him. Her dark eyelashes fluttering, she smiled, and nodded yes. They married during Shrovetide just before Lent. He was startled to see that she wore her red cloak over her wedding dress. It floated around her, and her dark hair streamed out in the wind.

Once they were married, Andrew took charge of her wardrobe. She demurred, but he pointed out that the Victorian head of household dressed his women to show off family wealth and that their social calendar demanded the correct attire. In April, he took her to Paris to purchase a new wardrobe that included several riding habits with matching jacket and skirt and a top hat and veil. Now she had morning dresses, walking dresses, dresses for the races and the opera. She had great hats, furs, choker necklaces and jeweled collars, which Alexandra, Princess of Wales, had made famous.

They returned to Dublin, and he proudly showed her off. To his dismay, he noticed she wore all her beautiful clothes with the red cloak. One day when she was out at the dressmaker, he hid it in the attic and surprised her with a long jacket and skirt for travel and a duster to protect her clothes from the soot and elements.

Pictures showing her superbly gowned figure at Longchamps or at the polo matches frequently appeared in the illustrated weeklies of London and Paris. But her mouth tightened more frequently; her eyes darkened more often; and her laughter disappeared. His once-passionate wife with her knowing sidelong glances became a gentle woman quietly caring for him. Her fun-loving spirit seemed to have disappeared, which pleased his mother, but he noticed that she never skipped stones or went barefoot now.

She just needed a baby or two he told himself. Some little Rigbys to carry on the family name and to bring the smile back to her face. His life was well ordered, but his wife was not. Some nights when the moon was high in the sky, she would leave his bed and wander to the sea.

By June, her hair lost its sheen; her eyes no longer sparkled. She spent hours in bed and when awake resembled a zombie. Andrew missed her boldness and way she used to laugh and joke with him. Late in the evening, Andrew would find her standing by the window looking at the last light of the day. When they were in the country, she would walk to the beach and gaze at the incoming tide. One morning she came to him, holding her old red cloak. Tears glittered in her eyes. "My coat, my coat," she gasped.

"Where did you find that?"

"In the attic. How could you hide it from me?" A pulse flickered rapidly in her smooth cheek.

Slowly, she wrapped herself in her old red cloak. Her eyes began to snap with joy. She threw back her head and laughed. Her forgotten laughter sounded like a whole caravan of sleighs, Andrew thought. She leaned over and kissed Andrew. "Goodbye, my love, it is my time to return to the sea."

Andrew never saw his love again. He walked the beach every day searching for her but she never was there. His life became quite dreary and dull, but sometimes on quiet starry nights he could hear her bell-like laughter.

Without our action or invitation, the dead often do appear to the living. We expect to find them in the ruins of homes, castles, churches, and other ancient buildings – such as those found all over the Irish countryside. They are from centuries past, and nature is steadily claiming them, but the spirits may still be present. *Courtesy of Ciaran McHugh*.

The Headless Horseman

Once upon a time, there was this tranquil town known as Kilcummer in County Cork. The rivers Awbeg and Blackwater ran through it. It had four fairs a year for cattle and pigs and less than 1,000 inhabitants. Its major claim to fame in 1837 was that poet Edmund Spenser's castle was sited there. In the long winter evenings, neighbors would gather by someone's fireside, the men would sip some whiskey, and the women would roast some chestnuts. Soon, one or two would tell stories and sing a few songs. The story they told most frequently was the one about the Headless Horseman, who was said to be the ghost of a horseman who was killed while racing his large stallion along the country roads in the area.

About five years after the horseman died, they said the local people began to see a headless horseman riding on a large stallion in the moonlit gloom. One old man with a long beard told of meeting the headless horseman one dark night. The horseman, he said, made him climb up behind him. They rode over bushes, hills, and swamps. Another said, "When he reached the bridge, the horseman suddenly turned into a skeleton and sprang away over the treetops."

An old woman listening to him nodded, "Ghosts and evil spirits don't cross running water."

"When it is dark and the only light comes from your lantern, you see all sorts of things you don't want to see on your path," added another. "One night I swore I saw a light rising from the graveyard and then a white misty figure burst forth..." he gulped. "I ran as fast as I could for the bridge."

One man coming home late one moonless night swore he heard the sound of hoof beats and the crack of a whip on the road behind him. Another saw the horseman in his dashing cape riding around the cemetery; a third saw him riding along the banks of the brook. The villagers said that he carried his head in his arms. A wise woman said that the only way he would leave the area was if someone beat him in a horse race.

Some people wondered whether they ought to stop going out after sunset. One or two insisted that not even church could get them to venture forth once the night had come. When they came home after work, they said, they blocked their doors. They draped their windows. They kept fires lit in the fireplace should the specter decide to come in through the chimney.

Now, the youngest laborer in Kilcummer was Tom Farrell. He had a tall, lanky body; long, thin arms; and big feet. His head was a small thing resting on his long skinny neck with its prominent Adam's apple. Although he was not very prepossessing, he had been raised well and knew enough to offer to help the other farmers with their chores. He would drive the herds to pasture, reap hay, plant potatoes, and help dig them up at harvest time. In turn, the farmers would ask him to share a meal with their families. Later, he would smoke a pipe with each farmer and his sons and flirt with the farmer's daughters. Sometimes a family and he would sit around the warm fireside and tell stories about this land of quaking bogs, bare and windy moors, and dark woods that ran down to the lonely, shining sea.

Tom particularly liked stories of haunts. The headless horseman had been seen several times of late, riding about the area and was said to tether his horse among the graves in the churchyard. People said to meet him meant death within the year. The only way to circumvent that was to outride him, which was impossible, and then they would tell stories of those who had died trying.

When it was time for Tom to leave a family's warm, cozy hearth, he would regret that he had listened to those tales of the supernatural. He took forever to say his farewells, and once he was on the path, every stick that snapped, every cold breeze, and every new shadow caused him to jump with fear. All the stories he had heard began to haunt his journey home. Then he would promise himself that never again would he listen to these stories of the supernatural – but of course he did.

Tom was pleasant to everyone, and he always flirted with the girls, but the one he fancied was rosy-cheeked Mary O'Hara, whose father was the richest tenant-farmer in the area. His meadows were lush with potato vines, his orchard had prolific fruit trees, and his cattle were sleek and strong. A marriage with the buxom Mary, O'Hara's only child, would make Tom a wealthy man. Mary O'Hara certainly was the unquestioned belle of the area. She had a way of lifting her eyes up to his, tossing her hair about, and smiling that made Tom melt inside. When her intended, Dan Clifton, saw her acting this way, he would grit his teeth in rage, although he didn't really think that Mary was seriously interested in gawky Tom.

Dan was Tom's opposite. Strong and muscular, he wasn't well read, but he knew how to ride a horse. He was always ready to come up with a practical joke or a prank that would make everyone laugh. He would slap people on the back, letting out whoops of laughter at someone else's expense.

One winter night, a most joyous party occurred at the O'Hara's house. The table was groaning with roasted turnips, cabbage slaw, and several varieties of cake, from plum to seed cake. People danced, drank, laughed, and told ghost stories. When Tom reluctantly left the warm fireside to journey home, the night seemed darker than ever. The owl shrieked, the trees creaked, and the moon disappeared behind a dark cloud. The ground was so soggy that it squelched with each step of his horse. The constant moan of the wind could be heard on the distant hilltops. Once he was inside the woods, its shadows closed around him, and the silence became ominous. Branches obstructed his path, and pine needles prickled his cheek. He felt the panic rising within him. He was certain that he was being pursued. Was that his breath rasping or the thrash of foliage as his stalker gained ground?

Suddenly, Tom heard a horrible neighing and the sound of a great horse galloping behind him. He felt his fear rising up his spine and over the back of his head. A horrible cold fright came over him, and he found himself gasping for breath. Spurring his horse onward, he quickened his own pace. All was quiet for several minutes, and then he heard the ponderous *clump clump* of hooves and another rider on a large black stallion pulled alongside him.

"Hello," said Tom.

The other rider didn't answer.

"I'm just coming home from the O'Haras. Were you there?" Tom asked.

Again, no answer. The night grew darker and darker, the stars seemed to fade into the sky, and driving clouds hid the moon. The only sound was that of hoof-falls and Tom's rapidly beating heart. Tom whipped his horse frantically; he had to go faster. The stallion's enormous hoofs thundered alongside. The other rider rode besides him, still not speaking. The road was a patch of darkness. When the moon came out from behind a cloud, Tom could see the leaves of a big tree quivering in the night wind. The hoof-falls of the two horses thundered. Suddenly, Tom could see his companion silhouetted against the moon. He appeared gigantic, wrapped in a cloak, but he had no head! Instead, it was tied to the pommel of his saddle! Tom whipped his horse into a frenzied gallop, but his companion rode right beside him. On they galloped, through the village of Kilcummer, Tom and the headless horseman right behind him.

"If I can just reach that bridge," thought Tom, "I am safe." Just then he heard the hoof-falls of the black stallion close behind him;

he even fancied that he felt the stallion's hot breath. Another snap of the whip, and his horse was upon the bridge. He thundered over the wooden planks to the opposite side. Tom glanced behind him and saw his companion pulling back on his horse's reins. Tom had beaten the headless horseman! The next day, he told the villagers the story and proposed to Mary. Within two months, a smiling Tom had married a giggling, happy Mary, and Dan had left the village to immigrate to the United States.

Some believe bridges, such as Headford Bridge, are haunted because they cover running water, which acts as a magnet for supernatural occurrences. *Courtesy of Ciaran McHugh.*

Skeleton in the Closet

The Hawthorne was blooming and fish were leaping out of green reeds in the river when Rathfarnham Castle held its annual ball. The dogs were growling, barking, and generally underfoot. Carriages, wagons, horses, and servants were standing around as everyone arrived to celebrate. The guests entered the estate through the Roman triumphal arch. Nicholas Hume-Loftus' uncle, Henry Loftus, the Earl of Ely, had transformed the fortified medieval edifice into that of a Georgian house. The villagers said that the Earl had been presented with an Eastern slave and ostriches. After dinner parties, the slave would ride the ostriches around the gardens to amuse the guests. No one knew if that would happen tonight at this ball, but everyone knew that there would be lots of excitement. Certainly, the crowd was dressed for the occasion. Lights festooned the terraces, and musicians from Dublin were tuning violins and harps. Many of the women were wearing silky dresses of red, yellow, and pink, and the immense light silk turbans from Turkey, which Lady Blessington had introduced to the ballrooms of Dublin. All of them were wearing jewels. Men wore brilliant uniforms, dazzlingly with gold lace and the regimental insignia.

Barbara, the younger Earl's daughter, felt drunk with excitement. Once everyone came in, servants began to walk around offering wine, roasted lamb, and fresh oysters lying in their translucent shells. The smell of the sea was mixed with that of roses. Music and the gliding of feet came from the dancing chamber.

Richard smiled down at her. "I'm going to write your father and tell my intentions."

"What will you say?" Barbara contrived to look up at him through her lashes with an artless coquetry. It was so wonderful to have so many men interested in her, she thought. She loved the thrill of the chase.

"I will say I love your daughter with all my heart and wish to make her my wife."

"And then?"

"He will say yes and we will marry and then I will take you to my home. And from there we will conquer the world." He took her hands in his and caressed them tenderly.

Barbara laughed, shaking her head. She didn't want to travel across the flat gray bogs to a world punctuated only by isolated manors. She liked it where she was. But he was all she had ever dreamed her prince would be: tall, handsome, and strong, with hair so dark and eyes so green. Her life seemed so exciting when she was with him.

Later, she saw Henry come in. He was tall with narrow cheeks, and his eyes shone so blue against his sunburned skin. He came straight towards her. As he strode towards her, Barbara felt his ruthless vitality.

"I came," he said.

She laughed up at him. "I see that you did."

"I will lay down my life for you," he said, looking her straight in the face. "You know I want you by my side." There was strength in his face and voice. Barbara could see Richard glaring from across the room. She knew that her father would make the decision for her if she didn't decide soon. For him, marriage was a transaction, a peacetime weapon for the acquisition of more land and extension of power. Love of one's spouse was entirely fortuitous.

Later that evening, when the night's dancing was done and the carriages had rolled out of the castle, a few couples who had stayed the night strolled in the early dawn or stood talking on a parapet overlooking the sea. The rivalry of the two men for Barbara's hand had afforded much amusement to many. They would say, "Did you see how he stares at her – he's blinded by her."

"Richard doesn't have experience enough to keep a young wife in line."

"Henry will never let him have her, anyway. A marriage with her would bring their families together."

Early that morning, Barbara heard strange metallic sounds coming from the Great Hall. Richard and Henry were in the middle of frightening swordplay, a dance of chance and skill. Their swords moved so swiftly that the eye could hardly follow. Both of them were breathing hard.

She ran forward, "Stop, stop."

"Keep back, Barbara," one of them grunted. The other circled and slashed at him.

"No, I cannot let you two fight." She ran between the two men. Their swords clattered to the floor.

"We can and we will. You can't decide between us. We will resolve that issue with our swords." Henry ushered her to the door.

"No, you can't. I will tell my father. He will stop you."

"No. We have to settle this our way," Richard said. "Here," he opened a closet in the hall. "You stay there; the winner will retrieve you." The two men closed the heavy door, locking it, and picked up their swords. Their dance of death began again as they whirled their blades around their heads.

The heavy door fell shut on her. Deep within the shadowy recesses of the castle, the closet was small, dark, and airless. Although she had grown up to the sound of swords, she had never heard the grunts of pain, the angry curses, or the moan of the wounded before. So she wept, pleading through her door for them to stop, to tell her what was happening, calling for her father. So she didn't see Henry in one graceful, deadly step stab Richard straight through his side, bringing his crimson red sword back out again. Richard fell to the floor, where he died, and Henry disappeared. Later, his body was found in the sea. People said he was so appalled that he had killed Henry that he went for an early morning swim and drowned.

More than a century went by, and no knew what happened to the gorgeous Barbara, belle of the ball. It wasn't until 1880 when the skeletal remains of a young woman were discovered in one of the hollow walls on the middle floor. The lady of the castle had the corpse's silk dress made into lovely cushions. Supposedly, the remains had been in that cupboard for over 130 years.

Many castles throughout the world are supposedly haunted. Within their towers and turrets restless souls linger, and the darkness grasps you in its cold grip. Now ruined, Moyne Castle was a sixteenth-century castle built on the Black River on the Mayo border. *Courtesy of Ciaran McHugh*.

Go Directly to Jail

I write it out in a verse –
MacDonagh and MacBride
And Connolly and Pearse
Now and in time to be,
Wherever green is worn,
Are changed, changed utterly:
A terrible beauty is born.

—W.B. Yeats
"Easter"

Built in 1796, the enormous spooky Kilmainham Gaol was a place of anguish, misery, and death. Today, it is listed as one of the top 10 sights in Dublin. The prison held not only many key figures from the last 200 years of Irish history and politics, but also criminals, women, and children. In those days, even children were sentenced to several months of hard labor for petty theft. The youngest is said to be a 7-year-old boy.

During the famine years of 1845 to 1848, the influx of country people to the cities was enormous. Since they couldn't find work, they had to beg on the streets. The government issued a vagrancy law, which made begging a crime. If you can't beg for food, you may steal, which some did. If they were caught, they knew that they would be fed in prison.

As the famine continued, the prisoners were given foods of poor nutritional quality and less food in general, which led to disease and death. The narrow, bare cells were intended for one prisoner, but frequently men, women, and children were confined together, up to five in each cell, often with only a single candle for light and heat. Finally, to cut their costs, the British government began transporting large numbers of convicts to various Australian penal colonies during the late eighteenth and nineteenth centuries. For over eighty years, more than 165,000 convicts were transported to Australia.

The Irish and the British had had a rocky relationship for centuries. By the time of the Great Famine (1845 to 1847), many Irish had lost all faith in the British government, believing that the government neither listened nor cared about their complaints and grievances. Seeing themselves as second-class citizens in the world's greatest empire, they wanted independence for Ireland and out from under British rule.

This thinking led to the armed Easter uprising in April 1916 in Dublin. Irish republicans led the insurrection to end British rule in Ireland and establish the Irish Republic at a time when the British Empire was heavily engaged in World War I.

On the morning of Easter Monday, April 24, about 1,250 rebels set out to capture the most prominent buildings in Dublin. Dublin residents woke to machine guns. Troops were shipped from Britain, and martial law was imposed. The rebels hoped for support from the people of Dublin during the rebellion, but that did not occur. After six days of death and devastation, the rebels surrendered. On Sunday, April 30th, the rebels were paraded across Dublin as a jeering crowd watched. Damage to central Dublin totaled £2.5 million – a considerable sum of money then. About 500 British soldiers and over 1,000 civilians had been killed.

A military court tried the rebel leaders in secret and sentenced them to death. Fifteen men faced the firing squad at Kilmainham Gaol. One of them was the seriously wounded James Connolly, who was executed while tied to a chair because he could not stand on his shattered ankle. Their deaths were publicly announced after their executions, and their bodies dumped in a mass grave at Arbour Hill prison yard.

Before the Easter Uprising, few in Ireland openly supported the rebels. After the 1916 Uprising, those involved achieved the status of heroes, and their blood made Kilmainham Gaol hallowed ground to the Republic of Ireland.

Given this history, the Gaol has its ghosts. The government of the new Irish Free State closed the building as a prison in 1924. It stood empty for many years before restoration began. At that time, a resident caretaker lived in the former governor's quarters. His rooms overlooked the area where the gallows once stood. One night he noticed the chapel lights, which he had just turned off, were on. He walked across to the chapel, turned them off, and returned to his room, where he noticed the lights were back on. This continued three times that night. Lights going on and off, sounds of latches turning, and the soft scrapes of boots on stone do not make for happy caretakers.

During the restoration, a painter in the dungeon area was suddenly blown against the wall by a large gust of wind. He managed to fight his way out of the dungeon and refused to work in the jail again. Another volunteer was decorating the 1916 corridor when he heard heavy footsteps behind him. He was astonished to find no one there, even though the footsteps continued. Several children have paused, terrified on the threshold, refusing to go one step further, while one guide who was particularly susceptible to psychic sensations claimed that there was an evil aura around the chapel's balcony.

Restored in the 1960s, the Gaol now acts as a museum of punishment, as well as a memorial to all "martyrs" that ever spent time there.

The White Lady of Kinsale

Sailing, boating, and fishing attract the many visitors to Kinsale Harbour in Cork. Others like the selection of golf courses and the lovely walks, but Kinsale is renown for being the gourmet capital of Ireland. It also has a White Lady at the star-shaped Charles' Fort, built by the English in 1677, to guard the harbor from use by the French and Spanish in the event of a landing in Ireland.

In the 1600s, Colonel Warrender, a strict disciplinarian and commander of the fort, and his daughter, Wilful, lived at the fort. A strict authoritarian, the Colonel believed in rules and discipline. If there was a duty to be done, a task to be executed, the Colonel believed in doing it the right way – there was no excuse for mistakes. The only person he ever allowed to make a mistake was his beautiful, vivacious daughter, whom he adored. He knew that her engagement to Sir Trevor Ashurst would change their relationship, but he knew that he had to let the two of them marry.

The evening before their wedding, just as the sun was touching down on the horizon, the young couple was walking, hand in hand, dreaming of their future, along the fort's battlements. The sea was foaming like some great wild beast, the salt wind clutching at their clothes and Wilful's hair as she leaned over the wall to look at the water.

"Look, Trevor! " She pointed at some beautiful flowers growing on the ancient, lichen-spotted stones. "Can you get me some of those? They're so pretty."

A long way below, the waves threw up tall plumes of spray that crashed against the grim grey rocks. Trevor's face paled, and he visibly gulped. Sir Trevor may have been a brave soldier, but he did not like heights! The nearby sentry, who had overheard the conversation and was bored with sentry duty, volunteered to fetch the flowers. Sir Trevor took his place in the sentry box, donning the soldier's greatcoat, and the sentry began the perilous climb down the rocky cliffs to pick the flowers for Wilful.

The sun began to sink, and Wilful shivered in the cold evening breeze. Sir Trevor sent her inside to wait for him. For a while, he marched back and forth, turning smartly, and then resuming his pace. Time dragged on, and when the sentry still hadn't returned, Sir Trevor fell asleep.

When Colonel Warrender came around for inspection, he spied the sleeping sentry. He challenged him and received no answer. Furious, he drew his pistol and shot him through the heart. When he got closer and saw that he had shot his daughter's fiancé, Colonel Warrender was horrified.

When Wilful learned that her father had shot her fiancé – all because she wanted some wild flowers – she felt so guilty that she threw herself over the battlements onto the cliffs below. On seeing his daughter's body splayed on the rocky cliffs beneath the fortress, Colonel Warrender shot himself.

Wilful Warrender began haunting the fort in 1815, when Major Black, a veteran of the Peninsular Wars, saw a strange lady in an old-fashioned white dress enter through a doorway and walk upstairs. At first he thought she must have been one of his fellow officers´ wives, but there was something distinctively odd about her. He followed her, but she disappeared. On another occasion, two sergeants who served under Major Black, were packing equipment. One of the men was accompanied by his daughter. The little girl asked about the White Lady she saw smiling at her. Neither man saw anyone, but the little girl was adamant that she had seen a lady dressed in white, looking down at her. A children's nurse saw the same White Lady some years later standing over the cot of a young child.

In the 1870s, Captain Marvell Hull and Lieutenant Hartland were walking upstairs when they both saw a White Lady. She looked at the officers for a short while before disappearing through a locked door. The apparitions continued in the twentieth century.

Three people died because of a bouquet of flowers. The moral of this story is to never stand in for a sentry on duty.

The Norman deBurgo family of Galway built Shrule Castle on the Mayo/Galway border in 1238. In 1642, after a violent uprising the previous year, a large group of English Protestant settlers, led by Dr. John Maxwell, the Protestant bishop of Killala, surrendered to the Catholic forces in Castlebar and were later led to Shrule Castle. The Catholic forces are said to have killed many of the settlers. Some survivors of the massacre were taken to Ross Errilly Friary in Galway, where the monks cared for them. *Courtesy of Ciaran McHugh.*

One Day in June

Peter, Matty, and their baby, Emily, arrived outside the small Irish village around 11 o'clock that Saturday morning in June. The baby had been crying all morning. Peter wondered how stay-at-home mothers stood it when their babies cried and cried and cried. Emily just didn't look too cute to him today. Irritably, he insisted that they visit the Beltany Stone Circle on their way to town. "It's famous, Matty. They worshipped ancient gods there. We've come all this way from New Jersey, and I want to see it."

"Oh Peter," she whined. She absentmindedly rocked the baby, humming something off tune.

"I mean it, Matty. I really want to see it," he snapped. Matty was getting on his nerves, too. Maybe they shouldn't have taken the trip with Emily. His mother had said it was easy to travel with a baby, but he wasn't sure that she was right after three days on the road.

Matty stopped humming and was studying her hands with an intent expression. They both were silent. Then she said, "I'm sorry dear. I'm just tired." She patted his arm. "If you want to climb it, go right ahead, but leave me behind please."

"No way. This is supposed to be a great sight. I don't want you to miss it."

"Well, then you carry the baby. Maybe she will be quiet for you."

Peter felt pleased with himself when Matty reached the top and exclaimed, "Oh, this is fantastic. I can see forever."

"The guidebook says it is even older than Stonehenge. Feels quite mystical, don't you think?"

"Oh, someone else is here, Peter." From behind a rock came a tall, thin man with strange colorless eyes and a cadaver-pale face. "Welcome to our sacred spot," he said.

"It's wonderful," Peter said.

"Yes, we think so. Legend has it that this was a place of sacrifice, but then life changed." He looked down at the ground.

Peter shrugged, "Well, life has a way of doing that." He reached out and patted Emily's hand. "How would you feel about taking our picture here?"

The man stared up at the sky. "Look at that hawk," he commented. Peter stared up at the sky and saw a large hawk swooping overhead. The man shook his head. "Hawks are interesting creatures. Why don't you three stand in the center of the circle? As they gathered into their family photo op, the man continued, "You know the town is celebrating the summer solstice; you should join in. All sorts of games and food. You will see how we celebrate this time of year."

Peter said, "Let's go. We need some fun."

The sun was blazing yellow in the deep blue sky. They drove through the rich agricultural fields surrounding the town until they reached the center where they parked the car. The music, the talking, and the laughing crowds invigorated Peter. The three of them had been alone in the car for several days. Now, they were surrounded with families, children, joggers, and bicyclists. There was the snap of 22s from a shooting gallery, the crowd noises from the ring toss, the hoarse cry of sideshow barkers, the barking of dogs, and the snoring moo of someone's prize cow. There was noise, excitement, and hubbub; there were casting and fly tying displays. In one area, a man was displaying his hawks; Peter stopped to read his poster advertising the falcon flights in the afternoon. One bird sitting on a peg curled his sharp talons as Peter gazed at his hooked beak. There were gundog demonstrations, archery and air rifle shooting, horses pulling carriages, and a huge, tented village of food stands. Over the main street was a wooden arch with "Welcome to the Summer Fair" printed on it. Peter and Matty went to the Fine Food hall with its succulent delicacies, including honey and the bees that made it, a vast array of cheeses, meats, breads, game pies, venison sausages, dry cured bacon, and whiskies for sampling. He could smell sausages, grilled onions, manure, and hay.

Peter and Matty looked at each other. This was quite a fair for such a small town. "First," declared Matty, "I eat. I'm a nursing mother after all."

"And did you find what you want to eat?" Peter asked.

"Yes, the classic roast goose dish that man was advertising back there. I've never had roast goose, and I figure this trip is the time to try it."

"Good to see you getting your adventurous spirit back. If you get the goose, I'll have a venison pie and one of those lemon tarts that I saw a woman in the red-check apron selling. And perhaps we can swap tastes. Now's the time. Emily seems quite content."

"She won't be," announced Matty, "Once we stop and sit down."

Of course, she was right. Emily began to whimper just as they sat down with their food. Peter sighed. Fatherhood wasn't all that easy. But they found a quiet spot to enjoy their food and watch the bustling crowd. When they were done, Matty said she would continue feeding Emily and find Peter later.

Peter started walking in the direction of the biggest arena. Cows mooed and sheep bleated from various barns. He walked past the shooting gallery, past men costumed as North Irish Dragoons with muskets and sabers, past the penny toss, the strollers, gamesters, and midway gawkers to the big arena where he picked his way through the crowd between blankets and coolers, couples tangy with sweat, and groups of young men. The displays included the flying of hawks, buzzards, owls, and falcons. There was something about experiencing the birds of prey that fascinated Peter. When the hawks flew over the crowd, he could feel his hair ruffling in the breeze created by their feathers. The hawks flew back and forth responding to signals, and Peter found himself ducking as they came closer and closer. They were strong and quick in the air. Initially, they flew in from the west with wingtips almost overlapping. Rolling slowly to the left, one-by-one, they pulled sharply upward into a full loop. Their feathers flashed white sunlight in a great roaring shriek of wind. They were blurred grey shapes roaring out of a dive, flashing at many miles per hour past the crowd. Peter, like so many others in the crowd, stood with his mouth ajar. He noticed he could see their sharp beaks even at this distance.

Peter was so busy staring or ducking that he didn't even notice when Matty found him. She had put Emily in her backpack, and the two of them stood close to him. Matty's eyes were cast upward, and she was as overwhelmed as he was. The crowd was getting bigger. Peter noticed the men were gathered together – not speaking particularly. The women clustered in another quadrant. They talked more, greeting each other happily while beckoning to their children to join them.

The falconer called to his two helpers, who signaled their falcons to come on in. He now came forward on the stage. "Now's the time you've been waiting for."

The crowd quieted down. Children ran to join their mothers.

"Eagles have captured the imagination of the human race for thousands of years. Their place in myth, legend, and folklore is well documented, and in almost every part of the world where they come into contact with humans, they are revered."

People nodded, Peter noticed. The falcon master continued, "Now is everyone here?"

People looked around at each other. "I don't see Tom O'Kelly," someone said.

Someone else shouted, "He's left town. But what about Annie Clancy?"

"I'll bet she's still in bed," someone said. The crowd snickered.

"Well, go wake her," the falconer retorted.

"I did," said a female voice. "She's on her way." And at that, a pretty blond girl with long slim legs ran down the hill to where everyone was standing.

"You all know the rules. Whoever the eagle lands on belongs to the gods."

Matty's hand clutched Peter's wrist. "Peter, we need to get out of here. I don't like what's happening."

"Now, Matty, they are just country folk." He was too busy watching the falcon master opening up a previously concealed large cage. In it was a beautiful eagle – just like the eagle he had seen when he visited Alaska years ago. "Look at those wings – I'll bet they range from six to eight feet."

"I don't care about that. I'm scared, and we're leaving. We will meet you at the car." Matty turned and began to walk out – just as the falcon master let the eagle loose.

Effortlessly, the eagle circled in a strong thermal to a high altitude, then glided a long distance. Turning, it shot above the heads of the crowd, a grey cannonball in the middle of the area, and then it came back ever so slowly. Peter suddenly thought that the eagle was looking for somebody or something, for the bird cruised just above the crowd. It was so close that Peter could see the electric yellow beak and pale eyes, which reminded him of the man earlier this morning at the Beltany Stone Circle. The crowd was silent as they watched the eagle circle. The bird came to a complete halt and began to climb upward toward the sun. The crowd gasped. And then the eagle dove, plummeting from his position in front of the sun like a thunderbolt, back down to earth, where it landed on something at the fringe of the crowd.

"Ah," said the relieved crowd. "A baby and mother. Perfect." Peter heard Emily's screams as someone lifted the backpack off Matty's shoulders and then the crowd surrounded them – and they both disappeared.

When Peter couldn't find them, he raced to the Beltany Stone Circle but no one was there. His life had changed once again.

Ireland has an impressive collection of megalithic tombs. Carrowmore Stone Circle in County Sligo is said to be the largest cemetery of them in Ireland. The tombs are spread out over 3.8 sq. km (1.5 sq. mi) over a number of fields and town lands, most of them situated near the road. Approximately sixty-five monuments are left. *Courtesy of Ciaran McHugh.*

The Doyarchu

It is said that if you walk by the lake, you can sometimes see the Doyarchu. My neighbor tells me that he has seen it and it is as large as a crocodile, although I don't know where in Ireland he ever saw a crocodile – just on TV. He said that it surfaces as the sun sets, and you can see a break in the rhythm of the water as the setting sun shimmers off the surface.

I am old and tired. I have neither wife nor job nor children – not even my dog – to keep me fascinated. Life is no longer offering me anything. So I spend my days walking around the lake, staring deep into its depths, wondering whether there really is a Doyarchu down below – that if it wasn't just a tall tale told by old men to frighten small children. I have lived long enough and seen enough that I know there is evil in the world. And here in Ireland, magic still survives.

In a way, I am glad. If the world was Eden as God showed Adam and Eve, it could be quite boring—everything perfect all the time. Without evil, there could be no good. There would be no choices.

Doyarchus are said to have lived in our beautiful Irish lakes from the very beginning of time. Cuchulain, Oisin, MacCumhal, Fergus, and even St. Patrick knew of their evil. They attack by grasping their prey and dragging it into the water. Generally, they work as a team. Dogs and even small children have been their victims. In the past, the locals would declare the lake cursed and shun it. My neighbor told me that some locals sacrificed to the lake, feeding it with small animals.

Doyarchus are described as having one or more patches of white on them, especially a large patch in the middle of the chest. Their hindquarters are bigger than the forequarters and resemble that of a dog, especially a powerfully built wolfhound. The paws are big in proportion to the rest of the body, just as we would expect in an aquatic mammal. The head is sleek and looks much like an otter's, the neck is long, and the tail is long and slender with a possible tuft at the end.

As I said, I am old and tired, so I just sit by the lake, watching for the indistinct flicker of movement beneath its surface. Although there is no breeze, the murky lake does move, currents and eddies shifting. No creature lives close to the lake. No bird or insect flies over it. The grass close to its banks is seared; the trees that grow near to the water are dying. All nature knows that it contains evil; I just want to see it for myself. As the sky darkens and night comes on, the ripples became more distinct. The wind has grown chill; the stars are popping out; the black waters are silent. Sometimes I think I see a dark head just level with the water.

I load my rifle. I like my rifle. It bucks, and I can hear the slug make its high-pitched sound; all sound stops when it meets its target. Since the sightings describe the Doyarchu in a fairly consistent way, it could represent a real animal. Some cryptozoologists say it could be a new species of giant otter. Others believe that it is a variety of baby Loch Ness monster, although Nessie does live in Scotland – not Ireland. Another possibility is that it represents a link between seals and their terrestrial ancestors. Seals are most closely related to the bear family and the dog family. There was probably a primitive ancestor of modern seals that looked much like the Doyarchu.

Sometimes, for a brief spell, I forget. I believe everything is still all right. But it never will be all right – never again.

The Doyarchu had taken my favorite dog one morning when we were walking along the water. It had reared up and grabbed one of its legs. And my dog had looked at me with such pain in its eyes. He knew his end was coming and was hoping that I could save him. But I stood there like an idiot as the monster dragged him further and further in, and then he was dangling lifelessly from the Doyarchu's mouth. That was when I came to my senses and rushed to the edge screaming and yelling and waving my hands, but the monster just ignored me as it slipped down to the watery depths, back to its own kingdom, carrying my dog with him.

As I sit there, I can feel the atmosphere of brooding melancholia, which haunts the lake. I remember the tales of ghosts and spirits who snatch unwary travelers. I shiver in the chill of the autumn evening.

"Regardless of what it might have been, the lack of people seeing it today indicates that the Doyarchu, if it ever existed, is probably extinct now," my wife said. She has done a lot of reading. But, despite all her research, she was wrong. We were sitting on a wall overlooking the water, her hair was hanging down her back the way I like it, our feet dangling in the cool water, when it rose up in front of us, razor teeth bared. It reached for her, catching hold of her soft, smooth leg, pulling her forward and down. And she went, helplessly screaming. I still wake up hearing her screams cut off mid way.

It's almost midnight. I must have dozed off, but then I saw my son. We had gone fishing off Achill Island in the western coast of Ireland. We had salmon and trout and were chortling about our good fortune. No one had ever caught so much. The cloudless sky was dotted with tiny white stars shining high as we rowed towards home. Age 12, he was thrilled. He had hooked the bigger of the two salmon. We were talking about how pleased his mother would be if she had been alive. She would have bustled about skinning and gutting, talking about this dish and that, inviting the neighbors in. He was naming which eight people she would invite for his big catch when the monster had stuck its head over the gunnels and grabbed his arm. His weight had tipped the boat, and I was fighting to keep it level as it took my son. He left me wailing horror-stricken in a pool of blood and recently caught salmon.

I am alone now. Alone with the ripples of the Doyarchu. The birds have stopped singing as the moon rises above us. A dull clap of thunder muffles the sound of my rifle as I shoot at the monster. The shallow waters are lapping the meadow grass. It is time for me to go to join the others. I walk into the water.

Ireland is known for its beautiful lakes, such as Lough Talt in County Sligo, which is a glacier lake. Its mythology often populates these lakes with monstrous beings. *Courtesy of Ciaran McHugh.*

Hill of Tara

Author's Note

Located in County Meath near Newgrange, the Hill of Tara is an enormous site that has played a central role in the history, legend, and folklore of Ireland. Linked to the Stone Age and Iron Age, Roman times, and the rule of the Celtic kings, this hill was the coronation place of the pre-Christian kings in Ireland and considered the sacred place of dwelling for the gods. Lesser kings and chiefs came from every part of Ireland to enjoy great feasts, meet their friends and enemies, and listen to the music of the harp and to stories of the olden days. When the Celts invaded Ireland, the divine race of the Tuatha de Danann was driven underground to establish otherworld kingdoms. The Daghda, the chief of the Tuatha De, assigned each member one of these mounds or sidhe.

It is said that St. Patrick visited Tara in the 430s AD after lighting his "Paschal fire" on the nearby Hill of Slane. The kings appear to have abandoned the site in the sixth century, but it is still considered a major center of Irish spiritual and political heritage and the fairies are thought to live there.

The harp that once through Tara's halls
The soul of music shed
Now hangs as mute on Tara's walls
As if that soul were fled.

—Thomas Moore

I was driving to Dublin on M3 when I saw the signs for the Hill of Tara.

"You know, Moira, I'd like to just take a look," I said, but then I began to laugh. Here I was talking to my dead wife like she was with me in the car, but hadn't I buried her six months ago back in Massachusetts?

Losing my wife had been devastating. Who can I blame when my keys, glasses, or wallet disappear? Before, I would indignantly point out that I knew that Moira had hidden them, and she would just as angrily deny my charge. But I would know deep down, based on forty-four years of living together, that she was GUILTY. Who can I ask about what to eat for supper, or what shirt to wear, or what to do about the gas bill? Now I have to decide on my own whether I should:

- Keep the kids' old bicycle (crib, highchair), just in case I am presented with a grandchild;
- Take the snuffling, drooling, dripping dog to the vet or wait out this newest attack of growing old;
- Say yes to the wedding invite, when I know all the widows will besiege me.

And all those housekeeping questions? Do I really have to change the sheets once a week when I am only sleeping on one slim side of the bed and the rest of it remains untouched? Do I have to hang two towels when I use only one, but there are two towel rods? Do I really have to sit at the table to eat dinner or can I do what my mother said I never should and eat alone, staring absentmindedly at the TV?

My loneliness had gotten so bad that I'd decided to come to Ireland since I had always promised Moira that we would visit her grandmother's home. We were just talking to the travel agent when she came home with a strange expression, saying, "I got bad news from the doctor today."

The Hill of Tara had always been on our list, along with Galway, and Cork, and the ancestral home in Sligo. I snorted. I had gone there and found it just a car park. It really hadn't been a great trip. I still missed her dreadfully. Time for me to go home. The sun was about to set, and I still had to get into Dublin. But then my better half said, "But this is your only chance. You leave tomorrow night, and you want to spend at least a day in Dublin."

"Okay, let's do it." I talk to her all the time now. There's no one else to listen to me. She and the dog hear the funny story, my observations about the news, and what I think about life in general. Of course, no one else is around, so it doesn't really matter, and if someone sees me on the road talking away with no one in the car, they probably think I have one of those apps that my son talks about. Yes, losing my wife has been devastating.

Enough. I really want to see the Hill of Tara, at least just briefly. Think, over 142 kings are said to have reigned there in prehistoric and historic times, and St. Patrick himself stopped there.

There the magical Tuatha Dé Danaan lived. They had four great treasures: The first was the Stone of Fal, which roared when a true King of Ireland stood on it. It was later placed on the Hill of Tara, the seat of the High-Kings of Ireland. Then there were the two weapons, the sword, and the slingshot, both famed for their accuracy. And, lastly, there was a cauldron, which was always full of food. Ultimately, the Tuatha Dé were defeated, despite their magic sword and slingshot. Legend has it that they stayed in Ireland, but only in some mythic world. You can see how well I read the guidebooks. Not much else to do when you're traveling by yourself.

"Boy, Moira, the sun is beginning to sink – what can I possibly see? Maybe I can just get a feeling of the place. It's supposed to be steeped in spiritual mysteries. I can just hear her saying, "and to think we could be drinking a good Guinness and eating supper now; but no, you have to look at some fairy mounds as the sun sets."

When I got out of the car in this deep green landscape, no one was around, but I heard some pipes. I followed the music as the sun slowly settled in the sky. There was a circle of dancers, swirling and twirling at the far side of this giant stone. The setting sun seemed to explode in my face like a firework. Kneeling on the ground, I shielded my eyes with my hands. It was the same landscape, yet it had transformed into something different. The music ebbed and rose, ebbed and rose. The dancers made a wide circle and began to move, swaying and humming, bending and clapping. I was in a vast spinning universe. I felt so connected – I, who had never felt that way. The wind carried the dancers' hair streaming out behind them. I thought about joining in, which made me chuckle. I certainly had changed if I was thinking about doing something like that.

The sinking sun reddened the sky as they danced with abandon. Moira would have been right in the middle of all those dancers, I thought. She would have been waving her hands, kicking up her long legs and laughing. Suddenly, one of the couples broke from the group and started turning and whirling. Others followed, flinging their arms out, uttering shrill cries. The area was fraught with passion. A breath of wind lifted the leaves of the surrounding trees. The luminous sunlight became insubstantial, and something appeared to be moving within the shadows.

Down the path through the creaking ancient trees came a long-limbed blond. Moira stood over me. "Hey there, honey. I missed you." She reached out a hand. "Come walk with me and tell me how you are."

We walked and talked. The sun was low, burning gold through the trees, casting our long, distorted shadows on the ground before us. Branches swayed and creaked, and invisible night creatures began to stir in the dark. Then, the moon came up, and everything became silent and strange. There was no wind, not a bird sang, not a leaf stirred. There was no sound but the crunch of our shoes on the gravel path and the whistle of the wind in the trees. We continued walking, talking quietly. As the birds began to rustle and the grey chilly dawn appeared out of the midnight blackness, we reached an empty lot.

Moira said, "I have to go."

"No," I said.

"You are keeping me from my rest when you act like this." Fatigue and pain marked her face.

" Are you okay?" I asked gently.

"Not really," she whispered. This was my cue. I should take her into my arms; it was the moment I'd been waiting for. The moment I used to dream about that first month when I'd get into the empty bed and think there was nothing left. But I merely nodded compassionately. Passion stirred, for old times, for memories' sake, and then disappeared.

"It's time for me to leave, and you need to let me go."

I buried my face in my hands and knew she was right. It was time for me to move on.

The Irish landscape sculpted over the millennia by both natural and human forces is steeped in myths, legends, and fairy tales, stretching back to the age of the Celts. Knocknarea is a large hill west of Sligo town in County Sligo. The high limestone hill stands prominently positioned on the peninsula between two bays. A cairn of loose stones is at the summit. Although it has not been excavated, some believe that it conceals a Neolithic passage tomb. *Courtesy of Ciaran McHugh.*

The Bold Irish Girl

In 1845, suddenly and silently, our potato crop failed. Not just ours, but Ireland's entire potato crop. Over 4 million people in Ireland depended on the potato as their chief food. People say that about 1 million died. Some died from starvation, but most people died from associated diseases such as dysentery and an outbreak of typhus. More than a million people fled Ireland. They risked their lives on long voyages aboard overcrowded ships to sail across the cruel sea to settle elsewhere – mainly in the United States, which promised them so many advantages.

I always have had these lurid dreams. I can remember Ma waking me when I was little, saying, "Hush now, Margaret. You are only dreaming." But these weren't only dreams – they were frightening nightmares of dead people flung on the side of the road, of great waves, of a girl my age holding my hand and the two of us laughing. When I told my Granny, she looked very thoughtful.

"What do you think, Granny?" I asked.

"I think you're 13 going on 14, and you have second sight."

"I do?"

"Your dreams are trying to tell you something. They're lighting your way."

"To where?"

"That, I don't know. We carry the past and future within us, in our bones. Your dreams are your destiny."

She was confusing me. She confused me even further when she said, " You must live with a person to know a person. If you want to know yourself, live with yourself."

Between 1820 and 1860, the Irish constituted over one third of all immigrants to the United States, and two-thirds of these Irish immigrants were Catholic. In the 1840s, as a result of the famine, nearly half of all immigrants to the United States are said to have come from Ireland.

The Potato and I

My family and I ate potatoes all the time. My family consisted of ten of us. Pa and Ma, me – Margaret, age 14; Thomas, age 12; Connor, 10; Sheila, 9; Maureen, 8; Kate, 7; David, 3; and baby Mary.

It seems strange looking back now, but in those days, we ate potatoes morning, noon, and night, usually with buttermilk or tea. We would eat them toasted brown in the bottom of a heavy pot and mashed in milk or with egg and butter. We would eat them boiled, peeling back the jacket and dipping the potato into a bowl of salt. Sometimes that was all we ate. To this day, potatoes mean comfort, family, and a thatched single-room cottage with a hard-packed earth floor and a turf fire in the hearth.

> Potatoes at morning
> Potatoes at noon
> And if I were to rise at midnight
> Potatoes I'd get.
>
> —Nineteenth Century Children's Chant

We lived in a small village outside Sligo, where several dozen one- and two-room thatch-roofed cabins clustered together. In the village, we had everything we needed: weavers, shoemakers, singers, musicians, and storytellers. In the long winter evenings, neighbors would gather by a fireside and tell stories of Ireland's past and sing those sad Irish songs, and the men folk would sip some whiskey. Pa once told me that the heat from the whiskey spread from the tips of his fingers down to the pit of his stomach, ending at the tips of his toes.

My father was a farmer who owned but a small spot of ground. He had a cow and some chickens and raised several good hogs out of an old sow each year. He grew potatoes and some wheat, which he sold to help pay the rent. My brothers helped him turn the earth with their spades and sowed the seed potatoes. I watched over my sisters as we tended the garden, scared birds away from the crops, and fed the pig, cow, and chickens. I did the wash and the sweeping out of our home. My Ma would make the stirabout and oatcakes and tend to the babies. My Granny would tell us stories about ghosts, fairies, and little people.

Then the famine came. Without potatoes, we were starving. Reluctantly, we ate our scrawny chickens, which meant no more eggs. Thomas and Connor would go to the river to search for crabs, winkles, and cockles. Sometimes they found a fluke. My sisters and I would head for the great meadows to seek out the button mushrooms, which came up overnight in small clusters of little white faces. We would look for nettles and blackberries, smudging our mouths and fingers purple while we filled our buckets to the brim. We did better than some of our neighbors because my brothers found bird eggs in the cliffs, and occasionally, during the winter, they were able to kill a bird or trap a rabbit. But we were still hungry. Little David suffered more than the rest of us; he had such thin little legs, and his eyes were so vacant. He looked like a little old man, all wrinkled and bent. By February, Pa butchered the cow because we had no food to feed her, but that meant we had no more milk. By April, we were eating old cabbage leaves, seaweed, and Indian corn. It was a long hard winter. Then, Granny died from the bloody flux.

We planted our remaining seed potatoes and managed to get through the summer months as we waited for the harvest. My brothers trapped mice, rabbits, and birds. I took my little sisters out, and we walked forest and fields looking for edible roots and weeds. One day, as I approached our home, I realized how desolate it was. No smoke curled up from the chimney. No hearth fire glowed orange through the windows. I found Ma was just sitting with baby Mary in her arms. The poor little thing was so puny. She kept whining for something to eat. Ma would put Mary's lips to her breasts, but she had no milk. So Mary would keep on whining. I took Mary away from Ma and dribbled some water into her mouth to hush her. Pa came home and just sat silently. We were all waiting for the potato harvest.

Some couldn't wait; they roamed the countryside in search of food and work. We shared what we could and gave them a place to sleep beside our fire. In August, we had a heavy rain; the potato plants withered and blackened overnight. Even those that appeared healthy, when Pa dug them up, soon melted into a stinking rotten mess. Ma cried and cried. Pa visited his friends and came back smelling of whiskey. I kept my brothers and sisters away from him the next day.

One early September night, Pa disappeared for a long time. When he came home, he just sat in his chair with his head down. Finally, he raised his head. "We need to leave Ireland and find our fortune somewhere else." Little Maureen and Kate began to cry.

"I can't pay the rent. We don't have enough food. No one has food. My friend, Patrick, told me people were even eating their dogs and cats."

"What about the workhouse?"

"They bury you before you're dead here. They just throw you into a mass grave."

Thomas drew himself up, "I don't want to go to the workhouse." Mary began to wail, but Mom ignored her and pulled out her rosary beads instead.

"Neither do I, " said Sheila.

Pa kept on talking. "People are getting sick and dying. The government tells us to bathe, to wear clean and comfortable clothing…"

"We don't have any. We sold anything we had." I replied.

"I know," he laughed bitterly. "And the officials tell us to eat wholesome nourishing meals."

Connor laughed, "Meals of what, Pa?"

Thomas added, "There isn't any food. We ate all the chickens. The cow is gone. We sold the hogs."

"But we have the sow still, " Connor pointed out.

"The fields smell like death," I added quietly.

"We need to leave. We don't have any money to pay the rent. All I have left to sell is our old pig. And now the landlords' agents are throwing families into the street. They're tearing down the cottages and running the families off the land."

"Oh, Pa. That's awful."

"Indeed it is, Margaret. Our potato plants have blackened and withered. Any potato I dig out of the ground turns into black mush. There's not a single good potato left. We can't depend on you kids finding berries and crabs all year long. A man can't feed his family on that. We need to go to America," he said. "There's opportunity there, and there's nothing left here."

Ma began to sob. Sometimes I think she has cried everyday since baby Mary came. "There's no more food to feed my babies."

Pa went over to her and rubbed her shoulder. "Hush now, Peg. We still have the sow. I can sell her."

"And buy us passage?" I asked.

Thomas jumped up. "I've seen handbills promising plenty of work and good wages in America. The advertisements say comfortable passage, economical fares…"

Ma sobbed. Three-year-old David sucked his thumb; my younger sisters gathered around me.

"They say there's bread and work for all there," I said.

"And maybe the sun shines always there, too," Ma said bitterly, bursting into noisy tears.

"Look, Peg," said Pa. "The potato crop has failed again. The cow and hogs are gone. We have nothing!" He banged his fist on the table. If we don't pay the rent, our landlord is going to evict us. We can leave Ireland or we can wait until we are evicted, and then we would have to find some sort of scalpeen to put over our head."

"Uncle Robert is doing well in Boston. Remember his letter, Ma?" I said. Ma was very fond of her younger brother.

Ma continued to sob in the corner.

"Why are you crying, my Peggy?" asked Dad.

"Because I would be leaving everyone here."

"But they can come, too. That's better than sitting here and starving. And we have family in Boston."

Ma just kept on crying. She was worn out with the baby and my little brother. That night we ate our remaining turnips with some stirabout. The window was misted over with raindrops. Inside, the air was thick with smoke from Pa's pipe and the peat burning in the fireplace.

I dreamed I was on a boat with many others. The waves were crashing against it. Then the boat was sinking, and I was hurling myself into the water. Crewmen began flinging chairs, baggage and packing boxes at us – anything that could float. I started swimming towards a suitcase. Mary drowned. I was glad when morning came.

Pa and Thomas took the sow and went into town to sell her and get us tickets. Pa came back elated. "We had enough money to take a ship to Canada."

"But I thought we were going to Boston?" I said. "Uncle Robert is there."

"It's cheaper for us to go to Canada, and we only got so much for the sow. Then when we are there, we will make our way to Boston. I have some money hidden away." He hugged me. "We're going, Margaret! It's our chance."

Thomas was very quiet. When I asked him what was wrong, he began to cry. "I saw a dead man on the road's edge, Margaret. I don't want to die."

"We won't Tommy, We're going to America."

"Not all of us, Margaret. Pa says we're leaving Sheila and Maureen behind."

I stared at him. "Leaving them?"

"He says they can stay with Aunt Colleen while we find a home."

The night before we left, we prayed the rosary, ate what was left, drank, sang, and danced. The priest gave us a special blessing. My brothers were excited about our great adventure, but I wondered if I would ever see Sheila and Maureen again.

The Journey

The next morning, we loaded our belongings onto a handcart along with baby Mary and my brother David. Ma often had to sit in the cart; she was too tired. The rest of us walked alongside on the rocky path. As we walked, we passed little groups of people bearing coffins on their shoulder. We passed the dead – in the huts, the fields, on the roads. One dead woman had a baby at her breast. Poor and hungry like everyone else on the road, we just plodded along in silence.

We brought bedclothes, blanket, pillows, and utensils for eating and drinking. We had a supply of oaten cakes baked so much that they were hard as stones. We also had some eggs from my Aunt, which were rubbed with suet and bedded on their ends in salt to keep them edible.

While we were waiting for our ship, we stayed in a crowded boarding house where we slept six to a bed. I met Maggie there. She helped fill the gap that my sisters had left. She was about my age, and, of course, we were tickled she was Maggie and I was Margaret.

Tossing her red curls, she said,"I'm on my own. I was the only one left at home, and then my Ma and Pa died from the Black Fever. I had nowhere to go. So I decided to emigrate!"

I could almost feel my eyes bulging. Here, I had this big family, and she had nobody. She continued. "I heard that people can get rich in America, and I thought that sounded very nice." She laughed.

I agreed. "Definitely. Rich sounds good. Our landlord was rich, and his wife always had the most beautiful hats. Sometimes, she brought us small presents from England."

"You were lucky. I didn't get any fancy presents, but I could certainly do with having money." She scratched her arm.

"Someone told me that we are going to travel over 3,000 miles. We're going to be like these bugs. Scratching out a living in a new land."

"I agree." She scratched herself again. "I scratch all the time now. My Ma used to say it is a bad hen that does not scratch herself." She picked off a louse. "What are these?"

"They're lice. See this red dot? That's what their bite looks like. "

"So what do I do?"

"Squeeze them, so you kill them. And check your clothes." I sounded like my Granny, I thought. She pulled out this black cake and began to bite into it.

"What's that? " I asked.

"It's called relish cake. It's made from dried blood and mixed with old greens."

Lonely and mysterious reminders of a rural past that stretches back
centuries, thousands of derelict structures can be seen across rural Ireland –
from small farms and crofts to lonely shepherds' cottages and even villages.
Courtesy of Ciaran McHugh.

Three days and many lice bites later, we were able to board our ship. Crewmen were hauling blocks and ropes; the sails were flapping in the wind. Peddlers were selling compasses and other equipment they said we would need aboard.

"Look, " shouted Maggie, " I can get a telescope so we can see our way."

I grabbed her hand firmly. "Don't you dare. They're just looking to take your last pennies from you. You'll need them when we get to Canada." *I sound just like my mother used to*, I thought.

Dock masters were giving orders. I could smell salty air and see large birds flapping overhead. What was really incredible was seeing all the pork, butter, eggs, and sides of ham sitting on the dock intended for the English people – food that the starving Irish people had grown to feed their rulers.

"How can we be starving?" Maggie asked. "Look at all that food."

Tickets in hand, we joined the long line of Irish emigrants carrying their few bags and pots and pans for cooking. We were leaving our country of corpses and heading for a new land. We were aiming for Quebec, Canada, although Pa promised that we would head to Boston once we got there. "No more Union Jack. No King or Queen. We are going to have a President in the United States."

"Where's Boston?" asked Conner.

"It's south of Quebec, which makes it warmer. "

"That's good."

"More importantly, it isn't British."

People were shouting out their goodbyes and God bless you's. There was crying and laughing, excitement and confusion, sadness and the knowledge that we would probably never see Ireland or our friends and family there again.

Before boarding, a doctor asked to see our tongues as we passed him. Then we were herded like animals onto the crammed deck. I took baby Mary from Ma, who looked like she was going to keel over.

Someone behind me said we were on a coffin ship, which I found rather frightening. I hoped my younger sister and brothers didn't hear the comment. When we pulled out, the spectators remaining on the dock cheered. We echoed their cheer.

Overhead, a flock of seagulls flew about. Ma began to moan, "I'll never see Sheila and Maureen again." I didn't know what to say.

Thomas and Connor ran about with excitement. Maggie and I held hands. "To the future," we exclaimed. We had become best friends in our short time together; I never had time for friends before because I was always caring for all my brothers and sisters.

We spent the first day cruising down the river, borne along by the tide, before the river burst into the ocean. On deck we had our last glimpse of the green hills of Ireland. It all looked so peaceful. Who would guess that so many people were dying there?

The crowded and dirty steerage section was in the deepest hold of the ship, lit only by lanterns. It had little ventilation – none when the ocean was rough – and the hatches were shut and there was no room to move about. We slept side by side on narrow wooden bunks and foul, straw-stuffed mattresses. Luckily, I had a top bunk with Mary. It wasn't much fun to be on a bottom bunk if the people above you were seasick. The ceiling was only about five inches above me. The toilets for women were located at either end of the steerage section; men went above deck. If anyone was sick in the dark, they had a hard time making it to the toilet. During the storms, when the sailors battened down the hatches and we were shut into steerage, people would shout, weep, and pray, "Help me, help me." I could hear the plea in their voices – their desperation, terror, and the shrieks of all their breaking hearts. The sea would seep in, timbers would creak, and people and baggage would be tossed about. One woman had her arm broken when a trunk slid into her. People yelled and screamed. It was bedlam.

The trip was supposed to take about forty days, depending on the prevailing winds, but in poor weather the crossing could take much longer. Our ticket promised that water would be doled out at the daily rate of six pints per passenger (children under age 14 would get half rations) and was to be used for cooking, drinking, and washing. If the ship was delayed, our ration might be less. We were also supposed to receive one pound per day of flour, bread, rice, oatmeal, or potatoes and twice-weekly distributions of tea, sugar, and molasses. We had to provide any other water or provisions.

The provisions were not distributed as promised. Many of our fellow passengers – Maggie being one – had relied on the captain's observance of the promises contained in our tickets. After all, the price included payment for the weekly provision of food.

When it stormed the second night, the ship began to roll and pitch. We were flung back and forth in the pitch darkness. Through the sickening stench of bodies, blood, and urine, I heard moaning, shrieking, and chanting. Someone was shrieking that God was angry. The occasional flicker of light through the deck hatch told me whether it was daytime or night. I heard others vomiting and smelled vomit. I shut my eyes and dreamed of the smells and sights of my home. I heard the cows mooing in the field. They contentedly chewed their cuds as their great brown and white faces looked over towards our grey stone yard. I saw Thomas and me milking, and all of us having supper together. And before it was dark, we all knelt to say the rosary.

Another child died from dysentery. On a beautiful sunny day, the child was sewn up in cloth, along with a great stone, and flung into the sea. So far five people had died within twenty-four hours. Ma seemed to be doing poorly. When she walked, she tottered along. Her eyes were wild and hollow, and she paid little attention to anyone other than baby Mary, who looked all bones and eyes.

We were so crowded that many soon had ship fever from the body lice, diarrhea, and dysentery. When the hatches were open, we could go on deck in small groups. It was so good to get away from the terrible stench below. Connor was so excited when we saw a whale, although the crewmembers told us they were considered bad luck. Often sharks would follow our ship in the hope of finding a tasty morsel. In the first week, there were only a few deaths, but then the numbers began increasing. The bodies were wrapped in sailcloth and thrown overboard. The moaning and raving of the sick kept me awake all night.

Leaving Ireland was hard. There may not have been any food, but at least it was beautiful and green. Here all we had was water and the dismal tone of the foghorn. Children would ask for food from their mothers, who had none to give; men and women would groan or pray. When I wanted to cry, I went to Maggie. We supported each other.

Maggie was a great storyteller. She would keep me and the others amused often. One day, my sisters and I crowded around her in the stinking steerage and she told a story that was almost as good as my Granny's stories.

"One day," she said, "my friend, Tom, saw a Leprechaun with a pitcher of something. You know they say a body must never take their eyes off them, or they'll escape. So Tom kept watching the little man and finally he spoke to him. 'Maybe you'd tell us what you've got in the pitcher there?' said Tom.

'That I will, with pleasure,' said the Leprechaun. 'It's good beer. I know because I made it myself. Would you like a taste?'

'Of course.' Tom drank deeply, smacking his lips. 'But what I want even more is a crock of your gold.'

'So follow me,' said the little man. 'Come along with me, and I'll show you a crock of gold,' said the Leprechaun. 'You know Money swore an oath that nobody who did not love it should ever have it.'

"So off they went. Afraid that he would disappear, Tom held the Leprechaun tightly as they crossed the fields. Finally, they came to a great field full of potatoes. The Leprechaun pointed to a big plant, saying, 'Dig under that one, and you'll get your crock full of gold.'

'I need a drink first,' said Tom. Then he realized he didn't have a spade for digging. After another drink from the jug, he put a big *x* in front of the plant.

'I suppose,' said the Leprechaun, very civilly, 'you have no further occasion for me?'

'No,' says Tom, 'you may go away now, if you please. God speed you, and may good luck attend you wherever you go. But first give me one last drink.'

'"Of course and good-bye to you, Tom,' said the Leprechaun.

"So Tom ran for home and got a spade, but he was so tired after all that drink that he sat and napped before returning to the potato field. When he got there, all the plants were uprooted. So Tom realized that it is sweet to drink, but much can be lost while drinking."

"Good story, Maggie," I said.

"But it's just a story. You know when we get there, we will have to find work. I think I want to be what they call a Bridget."

"What's that?"

"A maid. That way I will get room and board and some money. I'll also learn how to act and live here in America. And then I will meet a man…"

"I know. You will meet the handsome son of the family. He will dress you in velvet and feed you roast lamb and—"

"I'll live happily ever after."

"And you will have a coach and four and three maids."

"And a butler! I've always wanted a butler."

When the ocean was rough, the water poured into the hold where we lay. We encountered a severe storm and had to stay in steerage for almost three days. The sewage and filth washed around our bodies, which were rubbed raw by the wooden berths. We couldn't stand because there was no room. We were down in steerage for two days and two nights, and the only light was from the hatch opening briefly,

I knew from the sounds of retching that someone near me was very sick. The smell surrounded me like a fog. Two men died of the flux, Their remains were placed in two sacks and they were dropped into the deep. No one mourned them because almost everyone was sick.

Finally, they opened the hatch. The storm was over. The sun shone again.

As I clambered to the deck, blinded by the sun, Maggie approached me. "Do you know that prayer that says:

May God give you...
For every storm, a rainbow,
For every tear, a smile,
For every care, a promise,
And a blessing in each trial.
For every problem life sends,
A faithful friend to share."

"Yes, my Granny used to say that."
"Well I said that to myself last night, and I thought of you."
I hugged her. Friends are wonderful.
"People died last night, Margaret."
"Where are their bodies?"
She pointed at the ocean. "I heard the sailors moving around early this morning and some great splashing."

Thomas came up behind us. "Maybe that means more food for us."

"Hush, Tom. That's a terrible thing to think," I reprimanded him. But when I looked at him, I saw the sunken eyes, the almost white lips, and the protruding bones. We were all hungry. Ma just shivered and stared into the distance. The baby had stopped crying. Pa was off with the men talking about what they would do in America. Sometimes the men seemed to do a lot of talking and not a lot doing.

Attracted by the smell of food, people hung around at the fireplaces, upon either side of the foredeck. These large wooden cases lined with bricks were our fireplaces, where we could cook our food. Many passengers just ate their food raw rather than waiting in line to take turns using the fireplace. They bickered, prayed, or just stood in line. Some made porridge; others and I heated oatcakes that had been cooked back home. Our main meal consisted of herring and potatoes. Some women looked like they were almost dead. Young boys were hollow-eyed and decrepit. If there were any wind or an argument between passengers, the ship's captain ordered that the flames be doused. So all those who had been waiting in line were left with cold or raw food.

People got sick and died every day. Baby Mary had died on the fifteenth day of the voyage. I gave away her clothes to a woman who asked for them. A crewmember put her in a canvas sack, and we said our goodbyes to her before they flung her overboard. Sharks were following the ship waiting for our loved ones. Maggie and I would sit on the deck, look at the waves, and talk about how it would be in America. She was determined to become a ladies' maid in a large elegant house. She wanted to wear a uniform, say "Yes, M'am" and save her money. I wasn't sure what I wanted.

Ma just lay in her berth, looking like a specter and wincing at the light. She no longer made any sense. Pa said he couldn't do anything about it and suggested that we all hold onto her and say the rosary. We did, but she didn't seem to hear us. Little Kate and David were looking poorly. Their eyes were large dark pools, and they couldn't seem to walk a straight line. I was afraid they would fall overboard.

At night, the number of bodies prevented any movement. People groaned, and I felt the spray of vomit from the woman on my left side. The girl on my right side told me that she had heard that one ship had caught on fire. So great was the heat that women jumped overboard with their babies in their arms.

I shut my eyes and eliminated my physical surroundings in my mind. I felt as if I was floating, weightless. I wasn't aware of the smell, the noise, the heat, or the dirt. I was nestled in my own world. Safe. Free. I saw my sisters Sheila and Maureen and wondered how they were. Faces floated into my mind: people from the past and present, a procession of silent images. Then the dream changed. The road signs were written in a different language, and I felt alone. I was like a stranger in a strange land.

When I woke up, I realized I wasn't alone. I had my friend, Maggie. I had lost many things in the past months, but I had gained something truly important: a friend on this dreadful ship that was running out of food supplies. People had the bloody flux and the "itch" from lice. Medical help was nonexistent, and the noise and smells of steerage were horrendous, but I had a friend.

Somehow we enjoyed ourselves. Maggie told stories. An Irish fiddler would play, and we would dance and jig on deck. And of course, we sang all those Irish songs. The women would sew and knit. Maggie and I would stare in wonder at the ocean.

Maggie had a rash. I promised her that despite my family, I would stay by her. We pledged ourselves to believe in this new land and a fresh start .

When we began seeing birds, a sailor said we had entered the Gulf of St. Lawrence. People thronged the deck, shouting "Glory to God" or falling on their knees to pray the rosary. An inspector in a big straw hat boarded the ship. "Ha, there's fever here," he shouted. We sailed up the river to Grosse Isle, the quarantine island. About ten immigrant ships were anchored there, waiting to be inspected. A stream of small boats carried emigrants to shore. Walking was hard after all that time on the ship. Many crawled to the hospital. On the ship next to us, the crewmen were lifting the dead out of the hold with big hooks and stacking them like firewood.

Ma and David were just lying on a berth. I tried to keep them clean, but there was little water. Finally, Pa brought a nurse to us. She shook her head when she saw them. She looked up at my father, "They have typhus, you know. I don't think they will make it."

Pa looked stricken. Then he said, "Do what you can," and he strode off with a frozen look on his face.

The doctor pulled Maggie out of line. "You can't go on until you get better. You have typhus." They put her in a small shed, where she lay with eight others. The rash crawled over her body; her eyes glittered with fever. I held her hand.

"Don't you go crying now, Margaret," she said. "If I don't make it, I'll still be with you. Don't you dare stand at my grave and weep. I will be like the sunlight on your face or the star at night. I will still be with you."

Ma, David, and Maggie died and went into the same common grave. My first real friend had wanted to find a fortune in the New World, but all she found was a grave.

Although I knew that it made no sense, I was glad that they had each other. Maggie could certainly take care of Ma and David.

A New Country

As we traveled to Boston by foot and vessel from Nova Scotia, I kept hearing Maggie telling me that I needed to establish a home and find work. That if I went into domestic work, I'd get high pay, secure work, and a place to live.

The waterfront was a crowded, busy place with draft horses pulling wagons filled with goods to and from the brick warehouses; beaver-hatted men sporting blue tailcoats and black stocks walked to and from their counting houses. Grimy urchins ran about looking for work or spare coins. Our uncle lived in Cambridge near the river.

He worked at the massive brickyard between Massachusetts Avenue and Alewife Brook. We moved in with him in a shack tucked into a nook in an alley. Other tenements, pigsties, horse stalls, and one overflowing privy surrounded us. The place had no light and little air. It reminded me of steerage. I had escaped from that, I told myself, so I could escape from here.

My uncle said, "It will be hard to get a job. You will have to take whatever work you can get."

"I thought this was the land of plenty," whined Connor.

"Plenty if you're not Irish Catholic. You'll take the jobs that the others don't want."

"What if I don't want to?" Pa hit him, and he hushed.

My uncle said, "Many employers refuse to hire the Irish. They put signs in their windows and advertisements that read 'NINA,' which means, 'No Irish Need Apply.'"

Pa said, "My back and shoulders are my livelihood. We have come too far not to get a job. We will get jobs."

And we did. Although we were in a strange country, we were with many Irish who were wrestling with the same problems. For the most part, the Irish did the heavy, dirty work of the city. My brothers and Pa could have been bricklayers, masons, carpenters, or plasterers, if they had those skills, but they didn't. Instead, Pa became a laborer who did the digging and laying of pipes for the city. With his big smile, Connor quickly talked his way into sweeping the floors of the neighboring saloon, and Thomas shoveled up horse droppings from the streets. On Friday nights, they would pool their earnings, and give me some money for food. We all lived with my uncle in a single room without a window that stank from the kerosene stove that I used for cooking, heating, and ironing. I took care of Katie and the cooking, laundry, and what cleaning there was, thinking I was too young to play Ma.

Then Katie died. We didn't really know what she died of. She was happily playing and then she began vomiting. Within hours she was almost dead. Now my large family was reduced to Pa, Thomas, Connor, and me.

I became a maid in an upper-class Yankee household in a large elegant house. There was no handsome son, but I liked the excitement of their family gatherings. Below the stairs, we had fun, and I made friends. Despite my Romanism, my employer respected me. When I asked for Sunday to be my day off, so I could go to Mass, they hesitated, but they gave it to me. I labored nearly twelve hours per day, six and half days per week, for an average weekly wage of $3.99, including room and board. I learned how to polish brass and silver, make tea sandwiches, shop in America, and cook the best of foods. Each month I sent some money home to my Aunt Colleen for Sheila and Maureen. Occasionally, Maggie would nudge me in the middle of the night. She would tell me that I could make it in this new world. In the morning, I would resolve again to have my own home and my own family.

Now that we had food on the table and something to eat, Thomas and Connor were working long hours in construction. We were known as shanty Irish, but we were making a new life – even a better life. Pa drank too much. Sometimes his friends would bring him home. And sometimes he didn't come home. He used his fists on Thomas and Connor sometimes, but he left me alone.

I tried talking to him, but my stalwart Pa had disappeared. Instead, he would wax sentimental. "It is a serious moment in a man's life when he says farewell to beautiful Ireland forever. We took a perilous voyage, to be sure, Margaret, and we watched our loved ones die."

"Yes, Pa, but we're still alive, and we're making a living here. And Sheila and Maureen are still alive in Ireland."

"That doesn't suffice."

At church, I met tall and brawny Thomas McCarthy, a strong, tall ice cutter. He worked with Mr. Tudor harvesting ice in Fresh Pond to be shipped as far as India. He asked Pa for my hand before I knew he was going to ask me. We married in October. It is as they say, "If in October you do marry, love will come, but riches tarry." We had few riches, but lots of love – until he died.

We had four American children who lived. As I raised them, I told them Irish stories and sang them those melancholy Irish songs. I told them that education, a good appearance, and good manners would carry them a long way. I told them about the days in Ireland, my family, and my friend, Maggie. I told them that they were Americans – that they could do anything in this marvelous country, if only they worked for it. No one was going to give them a pot for gold for nothing. They had to use their own brains to get it. And I told them the stories that Maggie had told me. They liked the story of the leprechaun best of all.

They all finished school and had good lives. My oldest, Patrick, ventured west to mine gold in California. My second, Neil, worked on the Northern Pacific Railroad in Dakota Territory. I worried about him the most because laborers had to blast tunnels through rock. They say that an Irishman was buried under every American railroad tie, but to the best of my knowledge he survived. My other two children stayed in Cambridge. James, who had been my religious one, became a priest, and my Maggie became a nurse. Now, she is getting married to a banker, who wants to own a turreted, towered, multi-chimney home on a large green-grass square outside of the city. He says that their new home will have room for me, and I can take care of their babies. In the night, my faithful friend, Maggie, smiles and hugs me.

Beginning in the 1840s, thousands of Irish immigrated to the United States to escape the widespread potato famine that haunted their country. Unlike earlier migrations, many of these people had little education and few skills. They had little money, few possessions, and were desperately poor. This sculpture entitled "The Great Hunger "is on the Common in Cambridge, Massachusetts. *Courtesy of D. Peter Lund*.

THE ARCHBISHOP'S LIBRARY

Narcissus Marsh (1638-November 2, 1713) was an English clergyman who was successively Church of Ireland Bishop of Ferns and Leighlin, Archbishop of Cashel, Archbishop of Dublin, and Archbishop of Armagh. Certainly, doesn't sound very ghostly. After the battle of the Boyne, he was made Archbishop of Cashel, and three years later, he became Archbishop of Dublin. In 1701, he founded Marsh's Library, near St. Patrick's Cathedral in Dublin. This public library was the only one in Dublin for nearly a century. He was inordinately proud of it, which is probably why he is occasionally seen deep in the stacks, looking through the books. But he's not looking to read them, but for a letter from his dearly beloved niece, who acted as his hostess and housekeeper. She was in love with the curate from Chapelizod, a picturesque Irish village within Dublin.

When she was a small child, he had taken her in after her parents died. He raised her as if she were his own daughter, giving her everything possible. Like so many proud guardians, Narcissus did not approve of her relationship. The man was only a curate after all. Although she tried to reason with him, her pleas fell on deaf ears, so she and the curate resorted to meeting secretly. They would leave notes for each other in certain books in the library. Their final note was to make arrangements for their elopement. They managed to get married and lived happily ever after, much to the Archbishop's chagrin.

The Archbishop's ghost is said to revisit this library named for him hoping to find these messages tucked in the elegant old books and stop them from their elopement.

The Love Story
of Breandán and Aislinn

One spring day, a good-looking young widower named Breandán buried his wife in the ancient churchyard of Truagh in County Monaghan. He had some money, a wagon full of his tools and goods, a cow, some chickens, a dog, and an old cat named Blackie, but he no longer had a wife. As he walked along the cliff path toward his solitary cottage, the drifting fog blotted out the sun and he told himself to hurry along. He didn't want to linger overlong along this path where fairies might be lurking. Suddenly, a beautiful woman with startling red hair stood in front of him. She clasped his hands.

"I'm sorry to disturb you, but you seem so forlorn."

Breandán felt the tears jump to his eyes at her sympathetic tone.

"Why not tell me about it." She looked up to him with an invitation in her eyes.

He began to blush and stammer, and she moved closer. She listened to him intently, smiling into his eyes and eventually her hands reached out to hold his. All about them in the forest grew darker as the setting sun disappeared and the trees on either side of the narrow trail took on threatening forms. Occasionally, a bird called to its mate or a small animal scuttled across their path, but they didn't notice as they talked. Branches swayed and creaked, and invisible night creatures began to stir in the dark. Then, the moon came up, and everything became silent and strange. There was no wind, not a bird sang, not a leaf stirred. There was no sound but the crunch of their shoes on the path and the whistle of the wind in the trees. Finally, she leaned over, kissed him on the lips, and disappeared. The rational part of Breandán's brain told him she was an illusion from the fairy world. It was just all the emotion left over from his wife's death. He began to shiver uncontrollably, and his lips tasted salty. He picked up his pace and soon reached his cottage.

Breandán plowed, cultivated, weeded, watered, and harvested. Some mornings, he would awaken and lie there warm and cozy in the rough homespun blankets while he considered the day. Then he'd remember. Half of him wasn't there and never would be again. His wife, who made him feel special, was gone. All he had was a few animals, and a demanding farm.

Then one day, a wagon pulled into his driveway. A slender figure with red hair was at the reins. "Hello, there," she said. "Remember me? I'm your neighbor from over that away," she waved over her head. "I am Aislinn Mander." She stared at him with piercing green eyes.

Breandán was stunned. She was real and she was beautiful. He introduced himself and invited her in. She said all the right things, and Breandán found himself laughing – something he hadn't done for a long time. She said finally that it was time for her to go and reached down to pat the dog, who backed away from her, his hackles rising. Breandán offered to see her home

"Oh, I can manage," she said, squeezing his arm. "I've been alone for two years now."

Breandán wondered if she was flirting with him. That little squeeze to his arm held the promise of something more, and he thought he had seen an invitation in her eyes.

The next week, Aislinn visited twice. Breandán began to change his shirt more frequently. He trimmed his hair. He washed his dishes regularly. Every afternoon, Breandán found he was waiting for Aislinn. He experienced a rush of excitement just thinking about the possibility of her visit. When she drove in, he was waiting for her.

"I brought you a teacake," she said.

Thanking her, he took the cake and took a deep smell. "Oh, it's been a long time since I have smelled something like this."

She smiled and caressed the inside of his arm. He broke off several crumbs and slowly swallowed them. "What a nice cake," he murmured.

"Nice as me?" Aislinn licked her lower lip expectantly. He took hold of her hand and brought it close to him. Immediately, she took hold of his hand and licked his palm while gazing up at him. Blackie yowled in the distance.

The following week she visited almost every day. Her large unblinking eyes watched him carefully, and her tongue flicked quickly over her lips. Her presence gave him a fierce energy. He cleared and planted another acre.

That May the trees burst into chartreuse leaf; birds sang melodiously in every tree and bush. By June, the blossoms were thick on his apple trees. Breandán found himself breaking into song for no reason and laughing and playing more with the dog. Life was good again.

Aislinn always came to his place but never invited him to hers. One day when Breandán had gone into town, he turned his wagon in the direction of her house, but he found that she lived down a lane choked with weeds and brambles and where clusters of strange toadstools sprouted. The ominous silence unnerved him, and he began to shiver with sudden cold.

When he arrived home, Aislinn was waiting. Breandán took her hands in his and lifted them to his lips, kissing each finger. Every cell of his body felt young, unencumbered, and as clean as the clear blue sky. He cupped her chin and noticed that her eyes were pupil-less. As he leaned forward towards her, Blackie hissed and yowled at his feet.

Aislinn stiffened and drew away from him. "Let's get rid of that cat."

"But I have had him forever."

"Yes, but if you and I are going to be together, we can't have a cat that yowls all the time."

"Blackie just wants to be patted."

"If you say so." Aislinn leaned down to pat the cat. Blackie sprang at her hand, breaking off one of her fingers, which spasmodically wiggled on the ground. Aislinn hissed and disappeared in a puff of smoke. All that remained was a lizard with a long tail. Brendan knew then that he had sold himself for a demon's kiss.

Sometimes trees can appear haunted. Perhaps they are.
Courtesy of Ciaran McHugh.

Alpha or Beta

When I was a little girl, my Irish grandmother used to tell me all sorts of stories. She would tell me stories about witches, fairies, selkies, kelpies, and the occasional black dog. "If a man shall meet a black dog once, it shall be for joy; and if twice, it shall be for sorrow; and the third time, he shall die," she would say. Of course, I never wanted to meet a black dog when I was little. But as I got older, I knew that was just another one of her sayings. She told me that if you see a black dog in Ireland you are going to die, particularly if you see it in a graveyard. If farmers hear the barking, they lock up their women so the beast cannot kidnap them and take them to a fairy home to supply milk for fairy children. I always liked the idea of a fairy home. Can't you see them all flying about?

My mother said since I could only get a part-time job my last summer at home before I went to college that I should be responsible for walking Zeke, my beloved golden retriever. She said I could do it anytime during the day I wanted to, but I had to do it at least once a day. Since I like to sleep late, I usually walked him in the late afternoon at the park down the street.

Zeke loved the walk. Usually, he ran ahead of me, probably hoping that around the next corner or behind the next tree he would find another dog to play with. Almost everyone knew him in the park: Nancy, the dog walker who had the great big white dog, Mo; my neighbor who owned Dexter, the black poodle that pranced and danced on two feet; and Tom, who walked duck-footed and was totally smitten by his golden lab, Nessie, named for the Loch Ness monster, he told me. It's a peculiar trait of dog walkers: they know the names of all the dogs but not of their owners. They were just Jasper's or

George's owner. We walked together, discussing the peculiar habits of our dogs. For me, I spoke of how Zeke would always jump in bed at 6 a.m., how he would cower at thunderstorms, how he ate a bar of soap one day and then puked up his Pepto Bismol—pink froth all over his ruff. When no one was around, Zeke found tennis balls – sometimes the ones that even squeaked—that belonged to other dogs – and brought them home. Sometimes he found a dead animal and would roll in it until I grabbed him. The park was his playground. He felt safe there, as I usually did.

I didn't like the park much when no one else was there. I remembered all those horror films, the first *Halloween, Alien,* and *The Shining*, the flapping clothesline in *Friday the 13th*, and I was just positive that something dreadful was lurking behind the tall pine trees. I knew those crows weren't just cawing, they were saying "stay away, stay away."

My mother would laugh at me and tell me my imagination worked overtime. "I knew I never should have let you watch those old movies. They just give you nightmares."

My father suggested that I write a story about what I imagined. "Maybe you, too, can have a hit terror movie."

I liked that idea, but I never got very far. I had many more interesting things to do.

So that summer, I worked at Pennys, plowed through my required reading list, walked Zeke, and thought about writing a horror story. Nancy and I became friends or at least we walked our dogs together. Both of us noticed the piles of short black hair that lay in the path occasionally. There was so much hair that it looked as if someone had really been combing their dog, but who would comb their dog on a dog walk path? By the time August rolled around, the grasses in the meadow in the park had grown so high that I could no longer see Zeke when he ran into it to retrieve his ball. The cicadas that had begun early in the morning in short rhythmic pulses were now a constant steady mechanical sound along the dried-up paths. The wind barely blew, and the leaves hung sadly in the heat. Within the woods, the light was thickening, stripping away the reassuring familiar world and replacing it with something more ancient. The birds didn't sing, and the sodden air muffled the sound of the insects. Fewer people came – probably because it was so hot, and Zeke and I walked alone more often. I rarely saw Nancy. When I did, she told me the clumps of hair were spooking her. Sometimes I thought I saw something hiding behind a bush or a tree, but it was always just a trick of the sunlight. I managed to scare myself just enough that I would make Zeke walk closer to me.

The last week before school began, the park seemed deserted. Zeke didn't prance and walked with his tail between his legs. I didn't meet anyone on Wednesday or Thursday. The piles of black hair lying on the path fluttered in the breeze. Friday, I took the trail I always took, but I had that eerie feeling that I was being stalked. When I looked behind me, I saw a large black dog with yellow eyes, ears laid flat against its head, and a blood-red tongue lolling from its mouth. It was just a leashless dog without a walker, I told myself. Everything was just fine. Zeke put his head down and whined. He certainly wasn't being very alpha today. The dog stared unblinkingly at Zeke and me. When I turned and looked again, he was gone.

When I mentioned the dog to my friends at work, they told me that it wasn't a real dog but a demon. That I would die soon, for I had seen "the black dog." Then they all laughed when they saw my face. One nice person just shrugged and said "Come on, girl; it's just a dog."

The next day we were walking, and again, I felt that I was being watched. I turned around slowly, and I saw the same dog. Just like before, he disappeared. That was weird. Two days in a row. Then that Wednesday, I saw him again. He looked more threatening, bigger; I thought I could see the salvia dripping from his fangs. And then I was spooked. A kind of dread rose from my stomach. I began to shiver. I knew I had to remain calm. The moment I let fear take over would be the moment I lost. But that was easier said than done. My heart was pounding, and I knew the thing following me was powerful, cunning, and hungry. This sense of inexplicable fright gripped me. The light went really weird, and the woods grew quiet, all of its creatures seemingly holding their breath in unison. It was as if someone or something had hit MUTE. My hat felt too tight. Some new bundles of dark hair had joined the others on the path, and Zeke clung to my side. A low growl froze me in place. Zeke's hackles went up. Another growl was even closer. The light was shifting, and the air was suddenly cold – like an early morning mist. I walked faster and faster as my skin began to prickle with fear. A stick snapped behind me. I risked a glance back. Part of me said I was being overly imaginative, that nothing was there. Another part screamed at me to run. I heard this snarl and then a growling and snarling. A cold finger of fear went down my spine. I panicked when I heard a low growl. The enormous black dog was running right at me. Its eyes, big as saucers, looked fiery red, and salvia was dripping from its mouth. Zeke and I ran and ran.

I never walked in that park again. I did some research and discovered that since the 1800s, hikers at the park had noticed a big black dog. According to legend, the first time someone sees the dog, it brings him or her happiness. The second sighting is a warning. The third time means death. Whenever we pass the entrance, Zeke's hackles rise and he begins to growl. He's an Alpha dog as long as he doesn't meet up with the large black demon dog.

People avoid graveyards such as Carraigin Graveyard after dark, for the spirits that linger there are often vengeful ones. *Courtesy of Ciaran McHugh.*

BOBBY

Bobby was named for his uncle, Robert Cooney, because his mother had nearly died when she was carrying him. She and her husband had fallen asleep, having left a pan on the stove. Just as the smoke became really overwhelming, Bobby's mother had awakened and seen her brother, Robert, come in the door, turn off the stove, and then leave. As she ran to the door to thank him, he disappeared. The next day she learned that Robert had died in a car crash in another city at that very moment. Of course, she and her husband named the cute baby boy who arrived two months later for his uncle Robert who had saved their lives. Nothing untoward had happened since then, but they often told the story of his birth.

Bobby was the only child and the only grandchild. At Christmas time, his Nana would present him with a stack of beautifully wrapped presents. He would tear through them tossing one outfit after another onto the floor.

"Another pair of pants, Mommy," he would shout. "Another T-shirt. Another set of LEGOS. Another puzzle."

Having decided that she didn't want to vie with his maternal grandmother for the best present , his paternal grandmother would give him what she called an experience: a trip to a movie, lunch at a restaurant, or even an actual show. Meanwhile, her husband would slip Bobby's mother a $100 check. "Put it in his savings account," he would growl.

Yes, Bobby was a great favorite with the family. Certainly, he was spoiled rotten – some might say – but he was quickly forgiven when he didn't eat his supper or refused to pick up his toys or lay on the ground screaming when he didn't want to go to bed. His mother would rush to him. "How about an ice cream, Bobby?" Or a new LEGO set or one time she even offered him a bicycle. Bobby was the first grandchild on both sides, and he knew how to manipulate both sets.

Sometimes, when she took care of him, his paternal grandmother would threaten him with the naughty chair. Then, he would stamp his feet and tell her, "I hate you; I hate you." She would leave in tears, and his mother would comfort him.

Every event in his life meant that all four grandparents were expected on the scene, often bearing gifts. Every cute childish saying, every drawing, was the source of much approval. When his grandparents were away, his parents would let him call them, and he would babble into the phone while they would *uh-huh* approvingly.

Bobby learned his letters and how to count and went to school with his friends. His parents bought another bigger house, bought a SUV, and entertained Bobby's friends' parents frequently. And everyone marveled about Bobby's progress in life and his future.

One Sunday, when the meal was almost ready, Bobby's mom went upstairs to change her clothes. As she came back down the stairs, she heard Bobby calling her, "Mom, Mom."

"What Bobby?"

"Come find me."

"Honey, your grandparents are here, and we are about ready to have Sunday lunch."

"Please," he whined.

"Bobby, I said I am busy. That roast beef has got to come out of the oven now or it will be well done, and you know what your father will say then," she snapped. *Honestly,* she thought, *he's becoming much too demanding.*

"Okay, you'll never find me," he said.

When Evelyn went downstairs, she saw Bobby outside playing on his swing set. *That's odd,* she thought. *I thought he was upstairs.* She asked her mother, "Ma, did Bobby just come downstairs?"

"No, dear. He's been out there playing for quite a while now. "

Bobby's mother felt uneasy. She could have sworn that she had heard him calling her when she was upstairs.

Once lunch was over, Bobby's grandparents went home, after complimenting Evelyn on the roast beef, kissing everyone heartily, and promising to return the next weekend. Bobby and his parents went to the beach. They brought the Sunday papers with them, beach chairs, and Bobby's favorite trucks. He started digging while his parents read the papers. They began to discuss a proposed tax increase and became quite involved in their discussion. Suddenly, Bobby's mother looked around. Where was Bobby? His truck was there, but he wasn't. The wind whipped her heavy dark hair around her face and into her eyes, stinging them.

Narrowing her eyes, squinting into the sun, she began shouting, "Bobby, Bobby." But deep in her heart, and with an unshakable certainty, she knew that Bobby was gone – gone forever. After all, she'd had a premonition of his disappearance.

LEGENDS

Guiness Schoolhouse. *Courtesy of Ciaran McHugh.*

POT OF GOLD

Probably, the leprechaun is the most common symbol of Ireland. He appears in ashtrays, mugs, and dishtowels. According to most stories, leprechauns are aged, small, somewhat irascible men who are cobblers. Small enough to sit comfortably on your shoulder, they are very smartly dressed in small suits, waistcoats, hats, and buckled shoes. Generally harmless to the general population in Ireland, they are known to play the odd trick on farmers and the local population of villages and towns.

They are reputed to know where all the ancient treasure of Ireland is hidden. Many of the stories about them revolve around their pots of gold.

John Kelleher was known to be a lazy man. He never had held a job; his fields were sodden and sticky with mud; the only things he could grow were weeds! He lived alone in a dirty, little mud cottage by the roadside for no one wanted to marry a lazy man.

Now John was a romantic. While his neighbors in the small farming community worked hard in their fields tilling, planting, tending, and harvesting, he spent his time dreaming. He certainly wasn't going to plant his fields or care for any animals. Instead, he thought of the day when he would be rich and have everything he could desire. He went to all the horse fairs, Saturday markets, and other meeting places, telling everyone that he didn't see why just the wee folk could have everything they want. As far as he was concerned, humans should have the same.

On this particular day, John was up early instead of sleeping late. He put on his only suit with his red silk tie. Today he planned to go to a local fair with sports, games, and dancing. He deserved a day's outing, he told himself. His neighbors might like to slave away over their fields of potatoes, turnips, and cabbages, but that wasn't for him. He knew that he deserved something better than a shovel and pitch fork in his hand.

He started to walk to the next town where the fair would be held. The sun was shining brightly, the cows and sheep were grazing peaceably, and the birds singing sweetly. He passed along the river; suddenly, he heard a strange *tap-tapping* noise from the other side of the hedgerow. He peered through the bushes, and there in the field sat a tiny little man with a red hat working on a tiny shoe. A leprechaun! John laughed out loud. This was the bit of luck he had been waiting for. Straightening his tie, he clambered through the hedge. The leprechaun waved to him.

"Good morning, John."

"Good morning to you, too, but how do you know my name?"

"I'm part of the wee folk, so I know everything."

"You do?" That's just want I wanted to hear." John stood over him.

"Stop looming over me, John. You look so threatening."

"What are you doing?"

"I'm making a pair of dancing shoes for the Queen of the Fairies."

"They're lovely," John said. "But I am looking for your pot of gold. Leprechauns have lots of money, and I want some of yours."

"If it is gold you're after, John, you won't find that I have any of it. That's just silly, John."

"I'm not being silly, little man." John reached down and grabbed the leprechaun by his neck and shook him like a rag doll.

"Stop that," screamed the leprechaun. "You're hurting me."

"I'll stop it when you give me a pot of gold," John snapped.

"You think I have a pot of gold?" screamed the leprechaun. "If I had a pot, I wouldn't be here working away while you're all set to go gallivanting to the fair."

"I want that gold," snarled John, and shook the leprechaun again.

"Let go of me," screamed the leprechaun.

"I'll let you go when you show me where the pot of gold is," yelled John.

"All right, all right. Let me down."

John dropped him clumsily in the dirt.

The leprechaun stood up, dusting himself off. Glaring at John, he hopped across to a nearby cabbage field. "Here. It's under here," he said, pointing to a cabbage in the middle of the field.

John groaned. The field was dotted with thousands of cabbages, and he would have to go home to get his spade. How could he tell one cabbage from another? Then he realized he was wearing his bright red tie. Taking off his tie, he knotted it around a stick and stuck it right next to the cabbage,

"I'm going home for my spade," he said. "Will you promise me that you won't touch that tie."

"I promise," said the leprechaun.

"You better keep that promise," John growled. "Otherwise, you'll be sorry."

"I promise," squealed the leprechaun. "No one will touch your tie."

John hastened home, found his spade, and rushed back to the cabbage field. When he arrived on the field, he stopped in horror. The field was a forest of sticks stuck in the ground; each one sported a red tie.

Dearg-due

Once upon a time, there was a lovely maiden known as Deargdue who was so beautiful that everyone in the region knew her. This made her father most happy. He was looking to better himself through marrying her to a noble family with bigger castles, higher positions, and larger wallets. With her looks, he said to himself, she should attract some wealthy lords. Unfortunately, she fell in love with a commoner. They promised to love each other till their deaths. They talked of when they'd marry and the children they would have. They named them and thought about what they would do in life.

When Dearg-due's father found out, he was furious. "How dare you look at a commoner! You're to be married to a lord."

The tears fell from her eyes like green emeralds. "I don't want a lord. I want him. We'll be ever so happy, just like in the songs, you'll see. I'll give you a grandson with golden hair, and one day he'll inherit all this. He will be as fierce as the eagle and as proud as the lion."

"Stop the weeping, child. I know what's best for you." Her father sent her lover faraway and swiftly arranged a marriage with a wealthy lord. There was a great party, but Dearg-due was not happy. She sat and sulked in her wedding dress, cursing her father and threatening vengeance.

Her husband was a horrible man, who ignored her completely and went off carousing with his friends. She was so unhappy that she drank poison and died. Her husband married again. Her father and siblings were too busy with their new wealth that they never visited her grave. The only person who mourned her was her young lover whom she had to give up. He visited her grave, where he told her how much he loved her.

Legend says that the following year she rose from her grave. Riddled with vengeance, she visited her father's house. Finding him sleeping, she leaned over him and placing her lips gently over his, she sucked every breath of life from him. She then visited her husband and lured him away to a quiet place. There she sunk her teeth into his throat and drank his blood.

With only one night a year to enjoy her lust, Dearg-due lured as many men as she could to their death and then returned to her grave. And so, the legend of Dearg-Due was born.

THE GIANT'S CAUSEWAY

Fionn Mac Cumhaol was no ordinary giant. He was the biggest and the strongest giant in all Ireland. He could jump over treetops, leap from one mountain top to another, and smash boulders with his bare hands. His voice could be heard for miles around. His job was building a bridge to Scotland. He split all the stones he found into splendid pillars and columns and then placed them in the ocean. Fionn lived with his wife, Oonagh, in the hills of County Antrim.

Giant's Causeway. *Courtesy of Paul Doherty.*

One day, a gypsy came to their castle with news for Fionn. He told Fionn that a Scottish giant called Angus wanted to fight him. Angus wanted to show that he was stronger than any giant in Ireland.

"How big is he?" asked Fionn.

"His shadow stretches from one border to another," answered the gypsy.

Fionn whistled. "That's big," said Fionn. He went back to work.

The next day another gypsy came to see him. "A Scottish giant named Angus has heard about your causeway, so he's building one, too."

"Maybe we can meet in the middle," Fionn joked, but he was beginning to worry that Angus might be a serious threat.

His wife looked at him that night and asked, "What's wrong?"

"What's wrong is this Scottish giant. What if he comes here?"

"So?"

"I have heard that Angus is the biggest and the strongest giant in all the world. He is twice as big as I am and twice as strong!"

"Don't you worry. I will take care of you."

Several days later, a messenger came. "Angus is coming the day after tomorrow. He wants to fight you at noon," he told Fionn.

"Yes, of course," replied Fionn. "Okay, wife, what's your plan?"

"Go and cut down a tree. You must make an enormous cradle."

Fionn stopped work on the causeway to saw, shape, and smooth a cradle the next day while Oonagh sewed giant baby clothes.

The next day, Fionn brought the cradle into their house, donned the baby clothes, and lay down in the cradle. Soon there was a knock at the door.

When Oonagh opened it, all she could see was two enormous feet with giant yellow toenails jutting forth. She looked up and up and up. *Angus is a very big giant*, she thought, as she stared up at his face that filled the entire horizon. His beard was stained with the blood of his victims.

From between his gigantic yellow teeth, there drifted a dead animal smell, "Does Fionn Mac Cumhail live here?" boomed a great voice above her.

"Yes," said Oonagh, "but he's gone this week because he went to capture another giant."

"But I've come to fight him," Angus said in a low rumbling voice.

His breath made Oonagh's dress flutter and flap like a sail on a boat. She shrank back into her doorway and told herself, *you are a brave woman, now. You can outwit this foul-smelling giant, even though he's a fearsome creature who must be the size of a small mountain.*

"You," Oonagh laughed, "must not have seen Fionn. You are much smaller than he is." Angus took a step toward her. Oonagh felt the ground shudder when his big feet came down.

She shook herself. She could not appear to be afraid. "Would you like to wait for him? I will give you a cup of tea."

Angus hesitated and then agreed. Stooping, he came in the doorway, blocking all the light. He sat down, and Oonagh gave him a cup of tea. They sat quietly.

Soon Angus heard a baby cry. He got up and stood over the cradle. "That's a big baby you have there."

Oonagh said, "That's young Fionn, our baby."

"How old is he?"

"Just six months," Oonagh said. "He's a strong healthy boy. When he grows up, he will be just like his dad."

Angus thought that if this is the size of their baby, how big could Fionn be? He shook his massive head slowly. Then he ran out of the castle as fast as he could. He ran across the causeway and did not stop until he reached his country. He was afraid that Fionn might follow him.

Today, if you go to County Antrim, you can still see a small piece of the causeway. It is called the Giant's Causeway, because Fionn Mac Cumhaill, the most famous giant in the history of Ireland, built it.

The Importance of Hospitality

Ireland has always been crowded with inhabitants and people wanting to settle there. As the population centers changed, towns and cities were deserted and disappeared or became irregular heaps of dirty and stone. One of the most notable sites is Tara, once the greatest and holiest city in pre-Christian Ireland. Today, it is filled with rocks and irregular mounds. Thanks to the archeologists, it has been found, but there are others. The Irish have developed many legends to deal with these long-gone villages and towns.

Lough Neag

The transparent blue Lough Neag is thought to be one of the largest and most beautiful lakes in Ireland. Even small pebbles on the bottom are visible. An old Irish story says that it was formed when Ireland's legendary giant, Fionn Mac Cumhaill scooped up a portion of the land and tossed it at a Scottish rival. He missed, and the chunk of earth landed in the Irish Sea, thus creating the Isle of Man and the Lough Neag.

Originally, Shane O'Donovan owned a castle at the south end of the lake. His castle stood on a high rocky cliff at its edge. A village had grown up in the shadow of the castle's great walls.

It was not a big village because Shane was a mean man. He was merciless in war, nasty during peacetime. He was feared by his neighbors and detested by everyone else. No one really wanted to be around him.

One day, God decided to see whether the Irish code of hospitality still existed. He sent an angel garbed in human clothing to check out his people in Ireland. Weary from traveling, the angel asked for a night's lodging at the castle. Shane O'Donovan refused his request and set his dogs upon him.

The angel went to stay with the village cobbler, who was said to be so poor that he only had one potato. The angel shared the cobbler's potato and slept on the cobbler's floor. When the sun rose in the east, he called the villagers together and led them to a nearby hill and told them to look back. As they looked, they saw the castle and promontory slowly separating from the mainland and beginning to sink into the water. When the wall of water was higher than the castle battlements, the angel waved his hand in a commanding manner. At that, the waves rushed over the castle, the O'Donovans, and all its inhabitants.

The angel gave the cobbler a few more potatoes in thanks for his supper!

The Demise of the City of Peace

Once there was a lovely little town called the City of Peace in County Sligo. A poor widow carrying her twins asked for alms and shelter, but no one listened to her plea. She went from door to door, but no one responded. At the end of the road through the village, she began to scream so loudly that all the villagers ran outside to see what caused this noise. Once they were all gathered around her, the woman cursed the people and their town. They laughed at her and strolled back to their homes chatting about the indignant woman.

But that night the brook running through the City of Peace turned into a torrent and the waters rose, drowning the inhospitable villagers. Today, they lie at the bottom of Lough Gara.

Some people are fascinated by claims of ghosts, spirits, and even demons, and offer "proof" of the hauntings. MacPhilibin's Castle barely exists, but if you are out in the countryside and visit there, some say you can feel the darkness. *Courtesy of Ciaran McHugh.*

LORE

In the 1500s, much of the territory under English control operated in an almost constant state of alert for raids from the native Irish. Some clans swore allegiance to the English crown and became Earls, adopting the new religion as well. Others remained defiantly Irish and Catholic. Both sides clashed incessantly, drawing on the support of clans and families on the lower side of the social scale. This is the remains of the Shrule Fort. *Courtesy of Ciaran McHugh.*

The Field of the Cutting

During the sixteenth century, the Irish indulged in constant raiding and ambushing, occasionally fighting a single battle, but not really fighting wars. From 1561 to 1603, however, the Irish undertook a series of campaigns against the English. Significant support often came from Spain.

In 1579, Pope Gregory XIII sent 600 Italian and Spanish troops, who landed in Smerwick, Ireland. The Pope had sent them to aid the second Desmond rebellion, but the English forces blocked them from linking up with the Irish. The Pope's troops then retreated to the fort at Dun an Oir on the tip of the narrow Dingle Peninsula.

In November 1580, the English, under the command of Earl Wilton, a Protestant zealot, besieged the foreign troops in a ferocious siege, and the Irish stayed decidedly neutral. The fort rang with the sound of swords and the scrape of steel against steel, the thunder of drums, and the terrified screaming of a thousand horses. Men grunted with pain, shouted for help, cursed, and begged for mercy. When the Spaniards ran out of hope and provisions, they decided to surrender, having been led to believe by the English, that they would be taken peacefully as prisoners. After setting down their arms, they walked toward the English army.

According to the folklore, the English spent two days decapitating 600 Italian and Spanish soldiers, lining them up in a nearby field known as Gort a' Ghearradh or the Field of the Cutting and cutting off their heads one by one. Some of the bodies were used for target practice, but most of them were tossed into the ocean. The heads were buried in another field, appropriately called the Field of the Heads.

Many of us think of Sir Walter Raleigh as a knight, explorer, and poet who was known for his courtly manners and reputed to have placed his cloak over a puddle in order to prevent Queen Elizabeth I from muddying her shoes. Although the latter is not confirmed, a cloak is included in his coat of arms. It comes as a shock to find, according to local tradition, that Raleigh was the man who lopped off most of the soldiers' heads. To this day, according to the news articles, children in Dingle are told that if they misbehave they have to "Seachain a' Raleigh" or "watch out or the Englishman will come for you." The poet, Edmund Spenser, who wrote *The Faerie Queen* later in life, is also thought to have been present.

On the anniversary of the battle, people in the region have heard agonized voices crying in Spanish. Skeletons occasionally are seen floating by, and the stench of rotting flesh is carried in the wind.

One farmer on the edge of the beach says that he has seen "umpteen" skeletons. He recently found a pair of heads buried in a shallow grave in a field next to the beach.

Black Irish

Many say that sailors from the Spanish Armada landed in Ireland, found lovely Irish women, and lived happily ever after. Researchers have found otherwise.

In 1588, King Phillip II of Spain resolved to invade England. One hundred and thirty Spanish and Portuguese ships amassed, and thousands of soldiers were sent to Flanders to prepare for an invasion. When the massive Spanish Armada slowly sailed up the English Channel, Lord Admiral Charles Howard and Vice-Admiral Drake stood back and watched the Spanish galleons with their high turrets. According to one legend, Drake calmly continued with his game of bowls, saying, "There is plenty of time to finish the game and beat the Spaniards, too." That night Drake pursued one galleon, which surrendered to him when its captain learned that his attacker was the fearsome El Draque.

Ashore, series of hillside bonfires spread the news of the Armada's sighting, and the militia rallied to defend the country. This network of "fires over England" still takes place today to celebrate coronations and royal jubilees. Supposedly, 54-year-old Queen Elizabeth I traveled to inspect the militia in Tilbury, as they prepared for the invasion force. There, she gave one of her famous speeches:

> I am come amongst you, as you see…in the midst and heat of the battle to live and die amongst you all…. I have the body of a weak and feeble woman, but I have the heart and stomach of a king.

The English commanders decided to let the Armada pass and to pursue it up the Channel. Several nights later, the English dispatched deadly fire ships into the enemy's fleet as it lay at anchor. "Devil ships," whispered the terrified Spanish sailors. In the resulting confusion, the remains of the Spanish army fled into the open sea. The following day, at the Battle of Gravelines, the great Armada was beaten.

The remaining ships attempted to return home through the North Atlantic, when violent storms drove them off course. Their ships pitched and rolled as they climbed the foamy heights of the waves and then descended into troughs so deep that they were surrounded on four sides by walls of black water. Gunfire had already damaged many; others were running low on supplies. Many of the Spanish ships were wrecked on the rocky coastline spanning 500 kilometers from Antrim in the north to Kerry in the south.

The prospect of the Spaniards landing in Ireland alarmed the English Crown, which outlined harsh measures for both the Spanish invaders and any Irish who might assist them. Most of the survivors of the multiple wrecks were killed on the beaches, and the remainder fled across the sea to Scotland. It is estimated that 5,000 members of the fleet perished in Ireland.

The Night the Kitchen Fell

Perched high over the ocean in County Antrim are the breathtaking ruins of Dunluce Castle in County Antrim. The castle majestically crowns the white rocks beneath. Under the dazzling white rocks lies the Mermaid's Cave.

Built by those master-builders, the Normans, in the thirteenth century, the castle is reached by an arched walkway that connects it to the mainland. Around the thirteenth century, the Earl of Ulster, Richard Deburgh, built Dunluce Castle on top of the medieval fort, which can be traced back to the early Christians and Vikings. His ghost is said to walk the castle on stormy nights.

In 1584, Sorley Boy MacDonnell captured the castle from the English, when his men smuggled him in via a basket hauled up its side. Several years later, a galleass from the Spanish Armada, the *Girona*, was wrecked in a storm off the Giant's Causeway. Local folklore says the victims were buried in St. Cuthbert's graveyard nearby Dunluce Castle. The cannon from the ship were installed in the gatehouses, the telescopes and celestial globes added to Dunluce's furnishings, and the rest of the cargo sold. Sorley used the resulting funds to restore the castle. Eventually, he pledged his allegiance to Queen Elizabeth I.

Years later, the Earl and Countess of Antrim took up residence at Dunluce Castle, furnishing the castle with saddles worked with silver and gold, breathtaking paintings of the zodiac, and many other worldly gifts. Dunluce Castle was said to have one of the finest, most brilliantly beautiful castle interiors in all of medieval Europe.

A thriving village of merchants, settlers, and loyal Irishmen soon rose around the bustling castle, and Dunluce became an important center of commerce. Then, in 1639, life in the castle came to a crashing halt with a loud bang. Part of the castle's kitchen next to the cliff face collapsed into the sea, taking with it the family's dinner, all the chefs, and every servant but a kitchen boy who was sitting in the corner of the kitchen that did not collapse. That was *it* for the Countess of Antrim, who refused to live in the castle any longer. She was *out of there*. Two years later, Dunluce Castle was invaded and its surrounding village burnt.

By 1690, Dunluce Castle was deserted. During the years following the castles abandonment, many visitors and passersby added to the castle legend, claiming that the castle grounds were haunted by ghosts and inhabited at night by giants, dwarfs, and other mythological creatures.

Of course, there are many ruined castles and homes in Ireland. Within their towers and turrets restless souls linger, and the darkness grasps you in its cold grip. The ruins of Menlo Castle sit on the banks on the River Corrib in Galway. The Blake family, who arrived in Galway with Strongbow and are said to have been descended from one of the Knights of the Round Table, built the castle in this location in 1569. The Blakes soon became one of the powerful Tribes of Galway, a group of fourteen merchant families who came to dominate all aspects of life in the city of Galway between the thirteenth and late nineteenth centuries. On July 26, 1910, a tragic fire broke out that totally gutted Menlo Castle. The fire claimed the lives of Miss Ellen Blake, daughter of Sir Valentine, the fourteenth baronet and Lady Blake, and Delia Earley, a servant working in the castle. *Courtesy of Ciaran McHugh.*

The Wail of the Banshee

You can imagine the dismay when people hear the wail of the banshees, as they wonder who might be the next to die. The banshee, who is always female, is said only to appear to those Irish families who are considered important in the Gaelic world. Some say that the wail of the banshee is a warning to get your affairs in order. Sometimes she is seen; sometimes she is not. Her wail always fills its listeners with an unfathomable dread.

James I and the Banshee

James I of Scotland received one of the more famous banshee warnings.

> When the Queen cried, "Catherine, keep the door,
> And I to this will suffice!"
> At her word I rose all dazed to my feet,
> And my heart was fire and ice....
> Like iron felt my arm, as through
> The staple I made it pass:
> Alack! It was flesh and bone – no more!
> 'Twas Catherine Douglas sprang to the door,
> Except but I fell back Kate Barlass.
>
> —From Dante Gabriel Rossetti's poem
> "The King's Tragedy"
> 1881

After eighteen years of captivity in London, James I of Scotland was free to marry his beloved Joanna Beaufort, the niece of the King of England, and to assume the throne at Scone on May 21, 1424. During the next twelve years, James initiated constitutional sovereignty in Scotland, crushing the power of the nobles and inflicting revenge on his enemies. Not everyone thought he was great. He made some of the nobles quite angry.

On his way from Edinburgh to Perth, an Irish banshee told him, if he "Crossed the Forth, he would never return alive." James disregarded her advice, proceeded on his journey, crossing the Forth, and arrived at the Blackfriars monastery accompanied by his wife.

One night, when the stars were sharp points of light and the air was cold and clean, James and his Queen Joanna and her ladies in waiting relaxed in front of a roaring fire at the monastery. Some were playing chess and others the harp when they heard tramping feet, angry shouts, and saw shadows lurching in the courtyard. One of the ladies spotted armed soldiers filing into the courtyard.

She shouted, "Your enemies are below, Sire."

A band of soldiers entered the chapterhouse in search of the king. The unarmed king, who was in nightdress, ran to escape, but the windows were barred. Moreover, the bar to lock the door had been removed! Using the fireplace tongs, the King wrenched up several floorboards and scrambled down into the space below. One of the ladies carefully replaced the boards.

Meanwhile, the would-be assassins had reached the door. Lady Catherine Douglas stuck her arm through the brackets where the bar had been, buying the King the necessary time to conceal his subterranean hiding place.

The soldiers burst into the room, snapping Catherine's arm in two. The queen's ladies hovered at a corner of the chamber crying and weeping as the soldiers began searching for the King. The soldiers looked for the King in the withdrawing chambers, under the cupboards, the chairs, and all other places, but they could not find him. Meanwhile, the Queen stood on top of the loose floorboards that concealed the King's hiding place.

As the soldiers went into the outer apartments, the Queen opened the King's hiding place and reached down to extricate him. Unfortunately, the soldiers chose that moment to return to that room. Seeing the open hiding spot, they rushed to deliver the fatal blow. Unarmed, James had no chance to defend himself as the soldiers took turns jumping into the hole and repeatedly stabbing the trapped King.

He should have listened to the banshee's warning!

Incidentally, Catherine, the brave lady in waiting who barred the door with her arm, was thereafter known as Kate Barlass. Her descendants to this day bear a broken arm on their family crest and keep the name Barlass.

An 1891 Banshee

Lord Rossmore was Commander-in-Chief of the Forces in Ireland. A Scot by birth, he had come to Ireland when very young, and obtained the post of page to the Lord-Lieutenant. He had been extremely lucky not only in his vocation, but in love. The lady with whom he fell in love not only returned his affections, but brought him a rich dowry. Her money helped him acquire the Mount Kennedy estate in Wicklow. There the aged Lord Rossmore became a friend of Sir James Barrington, a lawyer and member of the Irish Parliament. Rossmore invited Barrington and his wife to be his guests at Mount Kennedy.

At 2 a.m. on August 6, 1891, according to Barrington's *Personal Sketches of His Own Times*, Barrington was awakened by "plaintive sounds" outside his window, from a grass plot underneath it. He is said to have remembered the wail for the rest of his life. He awakened his wife, who heard it also. In turn, she woke her maid. The sounds lasted for more than thirty minutes.

Finally, at 2:30 a.m., Barrington heard a voice call, "Rossmore! Rossmore! Rossmore!"

At that moment, according to Barrington's servant, Lord Rossmore died. It wasn't until the next day that they learned that their friend and neighbor, Lord Rossmore was dead. Having returned late in the night from Dublin Castle, he had gone directly to bed. Then at 2:30 a.m., his valet heard him make a strange noise and found him dying.

Although Sir James was terrified by the wail he had heard, the Irish staff knew that Barrington had heard the Banshee.

Have you ever heard an odd sound in the dark or a weird whisper of the wind as you walked in the dark? Those sounds are even more terrifying when you pass a derelict house, church, or castle. *Courtesy of Ciaran McHugh.*

Ashes to Ashes

Built on the site of an early Danish chapel (1095), St. Michan's Church today dates largely from its 1686 reconstruction, but is thought to be one of the few churches surviving from a Viking foundation. Its organ is one of the oldest in the country still in use. Supposedly, George F. Handel played it when composing *The Messiah*.

The ancient church has interesting artifacts, but its gloomy subterranean vaults are what attract visitors. A visitor enters this world through two heavy iron doors that open onto a narrow stone stairway. The limestone-lined tunnel leads to an underground world of hovering shadows. Some vaulted cells are private and fastened with wooden or iron doors, while others are open. Through the iron bars in some, ancient cadavers in their coffins can be seen lying in a haphazard manner. Although many of these people died 500 years ago, their bodies have been preserved naturally in the dry air. These mummies have nails on their fingers, and in some cases, you can see internal organs through rips in the skin.

In one vault, there are four coffins with the casket lids off, exposing bodies partly covered with taut, leathery skin and a thick layer of dust. Three of the coffins lie in a row across the front, a woman on the right, a man with a hand and both feet cut off in the center – some say because he was a thief, others say it was so the body could fit into the coffin. On the left is a nun. The coffin along the rear wall is that of a Crusader. One of his hands is lifted slightly in the air.

The last room holds the coffins of John and Henry Sheare, who were executed by the British following the Rising of 1798. When their old coffins were replaced with new ones, it was discovered that the standard British punishment for traitors had been enacted: the bodies had been hanged, drawn, and quartered. The parish records were destroyed when a bomb went off in the nearby Four Courts in 1922, during the Civil War, which hampers research.

Of course, the crypt with its spiders and gruesome remains is quite frightening. Footsteps echo, disembodied voices whisper, and some say long bony fingers have grasped their necks.

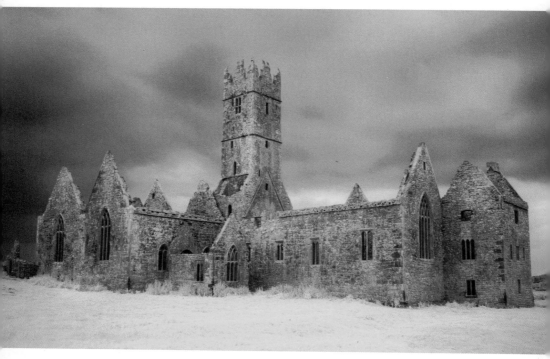

In 1348, Europe was in the grip of the Black Death. It is said that Archbishop MacHugh had a dream where he was told that in order for his prayers to be answered and the plague to end, he must first build a friary. He was told to go to Cordarra in Headford and that a sign would be given to him there. The next day, he arrived at Cordarra, where he saw three swans soaring overhead, each with a bunch of flax in their bills. The swans landed on a slight ridge near the banks of the Black River. When he reached this spot, the swans had disappeared and in their place he saw the three bunches of flax growing – all in full bloom, even though it was winter. The Archbishop took this to be his sign, and at this spot, he built Ross Errilly Friary.

In its anti-monastic crusade, the English authorities regularly persecuted Ross Errilly, imprisoning, banishing, or killing the monks. The abbey was finally abandoned sometime around the 1750s. By the 1800s, Ross Errilly was in ruins. Visitors to the abbey are said to have been greeted by significant amounts of unburied human remains strewn throughout the monastery. *Courtesy of Ciaran McHugh.*

BIBLIOGRAPHY

Corcoran, J. Aeneas. *Irish Ghosts.* Imprint: New Lanark, Scotland: Geddes and Grosset/David Dale House, 2002.

Crowl, Philip A. *The Intelligent Traveller's Guide to Historic Ireland.* Chicago, Ill: Contemporary Books, 1990.

Curran, Bob. *The Creatures of Celtic Myth.* London, England: Cassell & Co. 2000.

Curran, Bob. *Encyclopedia of the Undead.* Franklin Lakes, NJ: New Page Books, 2006.

Day, J. Wentworth. *Ghosts and Witches.* New York, NY: Dorset Press. 1991.

Fradin, Dennis. *The Irish Potato Famine.* Tarrytown, NY: Marshall Cavendish Corp. 2012.

Green, Miranda. *Dictionary of Celtic Myth and Legend.* London, England: Thames & Hudson, 1992.

Jones, Richard. *Haunted Britain and Ireland.* New York, NY: Barnes & Noble: 2003.

Jones, Richard. *Haunted Castles of Britain and Ireland.* New York, NY: Barnes & Noble: 2003.

Jones, Richard. *Mystical Britain and Ireland.* London, UK: New Holland, 2005.

Leavy, Una. *Irish Fairy Tales And Legends.* Boulder, CO: Roberts Rinehart Publishers, 1997.

Lethbridge, T.C. *Ghost and Ghoul.* Garden City, New York, Doubleday, 1962.

Levy, Patricia. *Ireland.* New York, NY, Marshall Cavendish, 1994

Lister, David. "Massacre victims from Raleigh's time return to haunt Irish shore." *The Times.* UK. April 13, 2004.

McAnally, Jr. D. R. *Irish Wonders.* New York, NY: Gramery Books 1996.

Newby Eric and Diana Petrie. *The Wonders of Ireland.* New York, NY: Stein and Day. 1970.

O'Brien, Maire and Conor. *A Concise History of Ireland.* New York, NY. Beekman House, 1972.

Reynolds, James. *Ghosts in Irish Houses.* New York, NY: Bonanza Books 1947.

Reynolds, James. *More Ghosts in Irish Houses.* Toronto, Canada: Ambassador Books, 1956.

Scott, Michael. *Irish Ghosts And Hauntings.* London, UK: Time Warner Paperbacks, 1994.

State, Paul F. *A Brief History of Ireland*, New York, NY, Facts on File, Inc., 2009.

THE WEB

http://zouchmagazine.com/architecture-abroad-the-east-wing-of-kilmainham-gaol/#ixzz1weTTGQvp

http://zouchmagazine.com/architecture-abroad-the-east-wing-of-kilmainham-gaol/#ixzz1weTTGQvp

Irish Wolfhound by A.J. Dawson. Animals in Irish History ww.irishwolfhounds.org/dawson2.htm.

Irish Wolfhound History. The Irish Penny Journal, Saturday May 8th, 1841, Vol. 1 No. 45.

Rein, L. M. Imprisonment of Women And Children In Ireland Had To Be Stopped. viking305. hubpages.com › ... › Ireland Political and Social Issues

RIP FerlinHusky. Fairwether Lewis. The Stones of Kerrigan's Keep March 17, 2011 by Faire Suzanne Barrett's "Ireland for Visitors." The Mummies of St. Michan's. irelandforvisitors.com. www.movilleinishowen.com/history/mythology/legend_of_the_banshee.htm

The ruins of Killaspugbrone Church lie at the most western point on the Coolera peninsula at Strandhill, County Sligo. The name Killaspugbrone means "the Church of Bishop Bronus" and relates to the original church which was founded by St. Patrick in the fifth century. The current ruined church dates from the twelfth century and is mentioned in the Annals of the Four Masters.

Supposedly, when visiting the site, St. Patrick lost a tooth, which fell out onto a flagstone and Bishop Bron founded the church on the spot. The Shrine of St. Patrick's Tooth or *Fiacal Phadraig* was made in the fourteenth century for the Lord of Athenry, Thomas de Birmingham; allegedly, this shrine holds the lost tooth. The shrine is now held in the National Museum of Ireland.
Courtesy of Ciaran McHugh.